Woman's Day
Old-Fashioned
Desserts

Also by **BARBARA MYERS**

GREAT DINNER PARTIES

Woman's Day
OLD-FASHIONED DESSERTS

Barbara Myers

J. B. LIPPINCOTT COMPANY
Philadelphia & New York

For my husband ROGER
and my daughter SYDNEY

U.S. Library of Congress Cataloging in Publication Data

Myers, Barbara.
   Woman's day old-fashioned desserts.

   Includes index.
   1. Desserts. I. Woman's day. II. Title.
III. Title: Old-fashioned desserts.
TX773.M94   641.8'6   78-15781
ISBN-0-397-01314-0

Contents

ACKNOWLEDGMENTS

I AM INDEBTED to a number of people for valuable assistance in the research that made this book possible. Mary Nickerson and E. W. Nickerson III provided a small library of early American and regional cookbooks without which I could not have succeeded. Important collections were also supplied by Mary O'Hanlon Bogard, Ruth Chenven, Wilda Jordaan, Martha Key Barnard, and Margaret Sadler. Others who helped were Nancy Aleu, Edward C. B. Bernard, Martha Brian, Nancy Conn, Lillian Hergesell, Sylvia Lustig, Mildred McDonough, Hedwig Mueller, Ellen Nickerson, Barbara Rau, and Ann Wellman.

INTRODUCTION

THIS OFFERING of old-fashioned desserts is a sampler of treasures from America's past. Though many of these recipes have roots that can be traced to origins in other countries, they have either been adopted by Americans or revised through the years. Other desserts are pure American inventions.

Writing a book on old-fashioned American desserts without delving briefly into American history would be an omission. The lineage of these desserts dates to the time when the first settlers came to American shores; it passes through the developing Colonial era and into the great period of American cooking of the nineteenth century. In this book it concludes about the middle of the twentieth century, when the approach to dessert preparation nearly succumbed to that of prepared mixes and canned and frozen preparations.

More than one hundred regional and old American cookbooks (particularly those printed in the 1800s) were consulted in selecting the desserts included in this book. A number of excerpts from these nineteenth-century publications have been scattered among the recipes. They stand as curiosities, but they also provide an insight to the difficulties American cooks confronted during past centuries.

This book is divided into six sections. Each category is preceded by a brief general history, followed by preparation techniques that may be helpful. Specific historical lore has sometimes been included with the individual recipes so that these recipes are more meaningful by being set within the context of their historical beginnings.

The recipes have been tested and adjusted to standard measurements, standard methods of preparation and cooking, and ingredients that are commonly available today. Only fresh or natural ingredients are required. There are no commercially prepared mixes or (with few exceptions) canned or frozen preparations.

Renewed interest in the American heritage, along with a basic desire to prepare foods from fresh and natural ingredients, has led to the publication of this book.

BARBARA MYERS

April 1978

I

Stove-Top Puddings and Refrigerator Desserts

THE DESSERTS in this classification were relatively late in emerging as part of American cooking. It was not until toward the close of the eighteenth century, when sugar became widely available, that puddings and chilled desserts began to increase in popularity. American cooks adopted the desserts of England and France and created variations of traditional themes from both countries. In fact, American contributions in this category are few in number, and those that have survived through the years are fewer still.

Some of the simple puddings remembered from England are favorite desserts today, especially those based on custard. But the more refined and elaborate old-fashioned desserts are adaptations of French specialties. Most of the French influence is creditable to the gastronomic interest of Thomas Jefferson.

Intrigued by French cooking, he returned from his tour as Minister to France in the late 1780s with a knowledge of, and a love for, the cuisine that was to dilute American dependence on English dessert traditions and thereby enrich the experiences provided by the final course of the meal.

Jefferson brought to Virginia society such rare ingredients as macaroons and vanilla beans. From his Monticello kitchen came blancmange, meringues, and soufflés, the first of their kind on this continent. His influence dominated dessert preparation for an entire century.

The original blancmange (translated as "white food") and several other French desserts required gelatin for their base. In the nineteenth century the only commercially available source of gelatin was the isinglass form, which was very expensive. In order to use gelatin, most cooks had to render the ingredient from calves' feet, a difficult and time-consuming chore. When gelatin appeared in the inexpensive granulated form, desserts with a gelatin base became a great deal more popular, eventually bringing about the commercial fruit-flavored gelatins of today.

The name "blancmange" was also applied to white puddings

made with cornstarch. When American cooks changed the color of blancmange by adding chocolate, brown sugar, or eggs, the name was dropped. Today we know these puddings as Chocolate Pudding, Butterscotch Pudding, etc.

About the turn of the century marshmallows (an American invention of the late 1800s) were being used in desserts, and a number of desserts were inspired by their use.

Around this same time, when wooden iceboxes were still being used, there was a category of American desserts called "icebox" cakes. These were prepared from simple uncooked fillings set in crumb-lined pans and chilled. Some of these recipes have persisted.

The current favorite among refrigerator desserts is cheesecake. Though its origin can be traced to the Roman Empire—and its similarity to the tiny British cheese tarts called Maids of Honor is hard to ignore—it is likely that what we now know as cheesecake was introduced to America by the early Dutch settlers. The Dutch made cheese pies with the equivalent of today's cottage cheese, which persisted as the main ingredient in cheese tortes (or cakes) well into the twentieth century. When cream cheese appeared, however, it quickly became the favored filling, probably because of its smoother texture. The popularity of cheesecake today suggests that it may have replaced apple pie as America's favorite dessert.

Custards

Desserts cooked on top of the stove (range) are often based on the preparation of a simple custard. Its base is milk or cream and whole eggs or egg yolks. The secret to the creamy smoothness of a custard depends on gentle cooking, constant stirring, and recognition of when it has thickened properly.

Custards may be cooked in a double boiler, which is the best way to ensure perfect smoothness and to avoid overcooking and curdling. They may also be prepared in a heavy saucepan set over direct heat. This method is quicker but trickier, and may take practice.

Here are some points to keep in mind:

1. If a double boiler is used, it is set over water that is barely simmering. The water must not touch the bottom of the top pan and must not rise above 165°, the point at which the custard itself will thicken. If a heavy saucepan is used, it is set over very low heat

throughout the cooking, or set over medium heat until the mixture is hot (140°), then finished over low heat.

2. The milk should be heated until bubbles appear around the edge of the pan, not until it boils. Part of the hot milk is poured into the egg and sugar mixture in a thin, steady stream while being stirred rapidly. This will gradually heat up the eggs and prevent them from curdling at this stage of preparation.

3. The custard mixture should be stirred constantly with a wooden spoon or a rubber spatula and cooked just until thickened. At this point the custard will coat a clean metal spoon with a creamy film that does not run off easily (165° to 170° on a candy thermometer). It must not boil, or the mixture will curdle.

4. Custards should cool to room temperature before they are refrigerated. If chilled quickly, they may thin out and turn watery.

Puddings

Unlike custards, cornstarch puddings and those thickened with flour must be brought to a full boil to thicken properly, even if they contain eggs.

Puddings made with flour must be boiled longer than those prepared with cornstarch in order to take away the taste of the flour.

To prevent a skin from forming, they should be stirred frequently during cooling or covered with a sheet of plastic wrap set directly on the surface.

VANILLA PUDDING

Vanilla Pudding, and those that follow (Chocolate Pudding, Butterscotch Pudding, plus Coconut Cream), are similar to packaged pudding mixes, but they taste better because they contain no additives and no artificial flavors.

½ cup sugar	2¾ cups milk
4 tablespoons cornstarch	2 tablespoons butter
⅛ teaspoon salt	1 teaspoon vanilla

Combine the sugar, cornstarch, and salt in a heavy saucepan. Gradually blend in the milk. Bring to a boil over medium heat, stirring constantly, then boil, stirring for 1 minute.

Remove from the heat and blend in the butter, then the vanilla. Chill, covered, to prevent a skin from forming. Serves 4.

CHOCOLATE PUDDING

Rich, dark, and bittersweet.

2 1-ounce squares unsweetened chocolate	¼ teaspoon salt
2 cups milk	1 egg
½ cup sugar	1 teaspoon vanilla
2 tablespoons cornstarch	½ cup heavy cream

Cut the chocolate into small pieces. Drop into a heavy saucepan and add the milk. Heat gradually, letting the chocolate melt slowly. (It will appear grainy, but smooth out in the finished pudding.)

Combine the sugar, cornstarch, salt, and egg. Gradually stir in the hot milk mixture. Return to the saucepan and cook over low heat, stirring until smooth and thickened. Boil for 1 minute, stirring.

Remove from the heat, cool slightly, then stir in the vanilla. Pour into pudding dishes and cover with a layer of unwhipped heavy cream to prevent a skin from forming. Refrigerate until well chilled. Serves 4.

BUTTERSCOTCH PUDDING

¾ cup dark brown sugar
   (packed)
2 tablespoons cornstarch
½ teaspoon salt
2 cups milk

1 egg
1 tablespoon sugar
2 tablespoons butter
1 teaspoon vanilla

Combine the brown sugar, cornstarch, and salt in a heavy saucepan. Gradually stir in the milk. (Any lumps of sugar will smooth out as the mixture cooks.)

Cook over medium heat, stirring constantly until the mixture comes to a boil. Remove from the heat.

Beat the egg with the tablespoon of sugar until light. Gradually stir part of the cornstarch mixture into the egg, then return to the remainder and cook 1 to 2 minutes longer.

Remove from the heat; blend in the butter, then the vanilla. Cool, covered, to prevent a skin from forming. Serve warm or cold in sherbet glasses. Serves 4.

VANILLA EXTRACT

Get 3 fresh vanilla beans of a druggist, break them in small pieces, and put them into ½ pint alcohol. It will be fit for use in a few days.

—Mrs. Owens' Cook Book and Useful Household Hints
by Frances E. Owens, 1888 Revised Edition (1884)

COCONUT CREAM

Creamy and soft, with only a hint of coconut for texture and almond extract for flavor.

½ cup plus 2 tablespoons
  sugar
4 tablespoons cornstarch
¼ teaspoon salt
3 tablespoons shredded
  coconut

3 cups milk
1 egg
¼ teaspoon almond extract

Combine the ½ cup sugar, cornstarch, salt, and coconut in a heavy saucepan. Gradually stir in the milk.

Cook over medium heat, stirring until the mixture thickens and comes to a boil. Remove from the heat.

Beat the egg with the 2 tablespoons of sugar until light. Gradually stir part of the hot cornstarch mixture into the egg, then return to the heat. Cook, stirring 1 or 2 minutes longer.

Remove from the heat. Cool slightly and stir in the almond extract. Pour into serving dishes. Cover to prevent a skin from forming and chill. Serves 6.

HONEY CORNSTARCH PUDDING

Blancmange, or cornstarch pudding, is a milk pudding thickened with cornstarch, flavored, and molded. It is the predecessor of packaged pudding mixes. This old-fashioned version is sweetened and flavored with honey, chilled, then unmolded and served with sugar and pouring cream.

2 tablespoons plus 2
  teaspoons cornstarch
¼ teaspoon salt
2 cups milk

3 tablespoons honey
Heavy cream
Sugar

Measure the cornstarch and salt into a heavy saucepan.

Gradually stir in ½ cup of milk. Add the honey and the remaining 1½ cups of milk.

Cook over medium heat, stirring constantly until the mixture thickens and boils, then boil, stirring 1 minute longer.

Pour into 4 small, fluted molds or custard cups that have been rinsed with cold water. Chill until set.

Unmold into dessert dishes. Pour the cream around the molds and sprinkle each lightly with sugar. Serves 4.

RICE PUDDING

Cooked in a double boiler rather than baked, this creamy pudding is dotted with raisins. It is served with butter, sugar, and cinnamon.

½ cup uncooked rice (not converted)	½ teaspoon salt
	½ teaspoon vanilla
1 cup boiling water	
3 cups milk	TOPPING
¼ cup raisins	2 tablespoons sugar
2 eggs	1 teaspoon cinnamon
3 tablespoons sugar	2 tablespoons butter

Rinse the rice in several changes of water. Place in the top of a double boiler and add the boiling water. Cook uncovered over direct heat until the water is absorbed (about 15 minutes). Stir in the milk and set over simmering water. Cook, covered, for 45 minutes, stirring occasionally.

Stir in the raisins and continue cooking 15 minutes longer, or until the rice is very soft.

Beat the eggs slightly with the sugar, salt, and vanilla. Stir part of the rice into the egg mixture, then stir into the remaining rice. Continue cooking and stirring a few minutes longer until the mixture thickens slightly. Do not boil. Pour into individual serving dishes.

For the topping, combine the sugar with the cinnamon and sprinkle over the hot puddings. Dot the tops with the butter. Let stand until the topping melts to form a syrup. Serve warm. Serves 6.

LEMON FOAM

From a simple sugar syrup start, this dessert is whipped until it is snowy white and attractive.

1 cup sugar	2 cups water
3 tablespoons cornstarch	3 tablespoons lemon juice
⅛ teaspoon salt	1 egg white

Combine the sugar, cornstarch, and salt in a heavy saucepan. Gradually stir in the water. Bring to a boil over medium heat, stirring constantly, then boil 1 minute longer.

Remove from the heat, cover, and chill. When the mixture is cold, stir in the lemon juice and add the unbeaten egg white.

Turn into the bowl of an electric mixer. Beat on high speed until the mixture turns white and looks like whipped marshmallow.

Pile into sherbet glasses and chill. Serves 6.

KISS PUDDING

The recipe for this golden pudding "kissed" with chocolate meringue comes from the cooks of the Amana Colony in Iowa. This dessert is also known as Pompadour Pudding.

¼ cup sugar	**CHOCOLATE MERINGUE**
4 teaspoons cornstarch	3 egg whites
¼ teaspoon salt	½ cup sifted confectioners'
3 egg yolks	sugar
2 cups milk	4 tablespoons cocoa
1 teaspoon vanilla	

Combine the sugar, cornstarch, salt, and egg yolks in a heavy saucepan. Gradually stir in the milk.

Cook over low heat, stirring until the mixture thickens and comes to a boil. Continue cooking, stirring for 1 minute. Remove from the heat and stir in the vanilla. Cover and chill.

To make the meringue, beat the egg whites until soft peaks form, then gradually beat in the confectioners' sugar and cocoa.

Turn the pudding into sherbet glasses and top with the meringue. Serves 6.

PEARL TAPIOCA PUDDING

Pearl tapioca is an old-time ingredient still available in specialty food shops, health food stores, and some supermarkets. When cooked, the tapioca resembles translucent pearls. This pudding contains chopped peaches.

2 tablespoons pearl tapioca	½ cup sugar
⅓ cup cold water	1 cup finely chopped fresh
2 cups milk	peaches
⅛ teaspoon salt	¼ teaspoon vanilla
2 egg yolks	

Soak the tapioca in the cold water overnight.

Place the tapioca (and any remaining water) in the top of a double boiler. Add the milk and salt. Set over direct heat and cook, stirring until bubbles form around the edge. Set the pan over simmering water and cook uncovered for 45 minutes to 1 hour, or until the tapioca is clear. Stir occasionally while cooking.

Beat the egg yolks with the sugar until light. Slowly stir the tapioca into the eggs, leaving the scum in the pan. Pour into a clean saucepan and cook over direct, low heat several minutes longer, or until the mixture thickens slightly and coats a clean spoon.

Remove from the heat. Stir in the peaches and vanilla and mix well. Serve slightly warm or chilled. Serves 4.

Note: This is a thin custard, like a pouring custard.

FLOATING ISLAND

This classic dessert can be made in several ways. One method calls for egg-shaped meringues cooked in scalding milk which is later used in making a custard. Another sets a single island of sweetened meringue on top of the custard, which is broiled until golden. A simpler version, and the one that follows, comes from Colonial times. The meringue is sweetened and colored with currant jelly and dropped into mounds onto the hot custard, then chilled.

4 egg yolks	**PINK MERINGUE**
¼ cup sugar	4 egg whites
1½ teaspoons cornstarch	⅛ teaspoon salt
4 cups milk	½ cup currant jelly
2 teaspoons vanilla	

Combine the egg yolks, sugar, and cornstarch in a heavy saucepan, stirring until creamy.

Heat the milk in a heavy saucepan until bubbles appear around the edge. Gradually stir the hot milk into the egg yolk mixture, then return to the saucepan.

Cook, stirring constantly over low heat until the mixture thickens slightly and will coat a metal spoon with a creamy film. (The addition of the cornstarch helps prevent curdling.) Remove from the heat, cool slightly, and stir in the vanilla. Pour into a warmed shallow serving bowl, preferably glass.

For the meringue, beat the egg whites with the salt until they mound softly. Gradually beat in the jelly and continue beating until stiff and shiny.

Drop the meringue by the tablespoonful onto the hot custard. Cool, then chill thoroughly. Serves 6.

TO ORNAMENT CREAMS OR CUSTARDS

Take the whites of two eggs, and two spoonfuls of raspberry, or red currant sirup, or jelly, and whisk them together one hour. Lay the froth in any form upon a cream or custard, piled up to imitate rock. It may be served in a dish by itself, with cream around it.

—The Improved Housewife, or Book of Receipts
by Mrs. A. L. Webster, 1854 Edition (1843)

CRÈME BRULÉE

Originating in England, and familiar there as Burnt Cream, this rich cold custard with a brittle sugar crust became known as Crème Brulée when it was adapted by the Creole kitchens of New Orleans. Before broilers came into general use, the sugar topping was glazed by passing a hot shovel over the top to create the burned appearance.

8 egg yolks	4 cups light cream
5 tablespoons sugar	1 teaspoon vanilla
¼ teaspoon salt	Brown sugar
1½ teaspoons cornstarch	

Beat the egg yolks, sugar, salt, and cornstarch until the batter is thick and pale and forms a ribbon when the beaters are raised.

Heat the cream in a heavy saucepan until bubbles appear around the edge. Gradually stir into the egg yolk mixture. Return the mixture to the saucepan and cook over very low heat, stirring constantly until the mixture is slightly thickened and will coat a clean spoon with a creamy film. (The addition of the cornstarch helps prevent curdling.)

Remove from the heat, cool slightly, and stir in the vanilla. Pour into a heat-proof shallow casserole or a 10-inch pie plate. (The cream should be no deeper than 2 inches.) Cool, uncovered, to form a light skin, then chill for a minimum of 4 hours, or overnight.

At least 2 hours before serving, rub the brown sugar through a sieve over the custard to make a layer ⅜ inch thick. Smooth with a spatula, making certain that all the custard is covered.

Slide the custard under a heated broiler to caramelize the sugar, leaving the door open to watch it carefully. It will take only a minute or so for the sugar to melt and bubble. After it is removed from the broiler, it will continue to cook and form a brittle crust. (The idea is a smooth glaze of sugar without a trace of burn.)

Return to the refrigerator to chill again.

To serve, lightly tap the glaze with the back of a serving spoon to crack it, then spoon out portions of crust and custard into sherbet glasses. Serves 6.

BANANA PUDDING

An old-time pudding recipe that was eventually adopted by commercial bakers of vanilla wafers.

½ cup sugar	3 large bananas (1 pound)
1½ tablespoons flour	
¼ teaspoon salt	MERINGUE
1¾ cups milk	2 egg whites
2 egg yolks	4 tablespoons sugar
4 tablespoons butter	½ teaspoon vanilla
2 tablespoons light rum	
12 ladyfingers or finger-size slices of sponge cake	

Combine the sugar, flour, and salt in a heavy saucepan. Gradually stir in the milk. Cook over medium heat, stirring constantly until the mixture is smooth and thick and comes to a boil.

Beat the egg yolks slightly, then gradually stir in the milk mixture and return to the saucepan. Cook, stirring 2 or 3 minutes longer, until there is no taste of flour.

Remove from the heat, add the butter, and blend in well. Cool slightly and stir in the rum.

Place a layer of split ladyfingers or sponge cake in a buttered 1½-quart casserole, add a layer of sliced bananas, then repeat, ending with bananas on top.

Pour the warm custard over the bananas. Set aside while preparing the meringue.

Beat the egg whites until they stand in soft peaks. Gradually beat in the sugar, then the vanilla. Continue beating until stiff and glossy.

Swirl the meringue over the custard, sealing to the edges of the casserole.

Bake in a 350° oven until lightly browned (about 15 minutes). Serve warm. Serves 6 to 8.

TIPSY PUDDING

Tipsy Pudding, sometimes called Squire Cake or Tipsy Parson, is similar to a trifle. A combination of sponge cake, custard, and liquor, it gets its name from its alcoholic ingredient, which may be sherry, rum, cognac, or whiskey.

Sponge Cake (page 76)	**1 cup heavy cream**
1 cup whiskey	**¾ cup blanched and toasted**
Custard (recipe follows)	**slivered almonds**

Carefully split the sponge cake into two layers with a fork and a serrated knife.

Place one layer, crust side down, on a shallow rimmed serving plate. Slowly drizzle half the whiskey evenly over the top. Let stand for a few minutes so that it is absorbed.

Cover with half the chilled custard. Place the second layer on top with the crust side up and slowly pour the remaining whiskey on top of the second layer. When the liquid is absorbed, cover with the remaining custard. (Part of the custard will seep into the cake; the remainder will spill over the sides.)

Whip the cream and place a mound over the cake, allowing the edges to show. Stick the almonds over the surface of the cream. Chill for at least 1 hour. Serves 8 to 10.

Note: If desired to hold longer, chill for several hours. Add the cream and almonds close to serving.

Custard

1 cup milk	**¼ cup sugar**
1 cup light cream	**¼ teaspoon salt**
4 egg yolks	**2 teaspoons vanilla**

Heat the milk and cream in the top of a double boiler until bubbles appear around the edge.

Beat the egg yolks slightly. Gradually beat in the sugar and salt. Continue beating until the sugar is dissolved.

Gradually stir the hot milk and cream into the egg yolks. Return to the double boiler and set over simmering water. Cook, stirring until the mixture thickens slightly and will coat a metal spoon.

Remove from the heat. Stir rapidly to bring down the heat, then stir in the vanilla. Strain and cool, then refrigerate until thoroughly chilled.

TRIFLE

Perhaps the most versatile of all desserts introduced into America by the English is Trifle, which could be prepared as simply or elaborately as the occasion demanded. The basics are stale cake, custard, fresh or preserved fruits, and whipped cream. Here is one of the more elegant versions, intended for a special occasion.

36 almond macaroons (7 ounces)	¼ teaspoon salt
1 cup dry sherry	24 ladyfingers
2 cups milk	Black currant jam
2 eggs	¼ cup broken pecans
½ cup sugar	2 cups heavy cream
	12 pecan halves

Crumble the macaroons into the sherry; let stand for several hours until the sherry is absorbed. Stir to blend into a paste.

Heat the milk in the top of a double boiler until bubbles appear around the edge.

Beat the eggs slightly. Add the sugar and salt and stir until creamy. Gradually stir part of the hot milk into the egg mixture, then return to the double boiler. Set over simmering water and cook, stirring constantly until the mixture thickens slightly and will coat a metal spoon with a light, creamy film.

Remove from the heat and strain the custard into a bowl. Stir to cool rapidly, then chill thoroughly.

Split the ladyfingers into halves and spread the flat side of each lightly with the jam. Line the bottom and sides of a 3-quart round glass bowl with the ladyfingers, jam sides up.

Pour the macaroon mixture over the bottom layer of ladyfingers. Pour half the custard over the macaroons, sprinkle with half the broken pecans, then top with the remaining custard and broken pecans.

Whip the cream until stiff. Spread over the top of the custard and chill for at least 1 hour.

Garnish with the pecan halves before serving. Serves 10 to 12.

TRIFLE

Put slices of sponge cake, or nice rolls, at the bottom of a deep dish, wet them with white wine, and fill the dish nearly to the top with rich boiled custard; season half a pint of cream with white wine and sugar, and beat it to a froth; as it rises, take it lightly off and lay it on the custard, piling it up high and tastily, and decorate it with preserves of any kind cut so thin as not to bear the froth down by the weight.

—The Improved Housewife, or Book of Receipts
by Mrs. A. L. Webster, 1854 Edition (1843)

COFFEE SPONGE

1 envelope unflavored gelatin
¼ cup plus 2 tablespoons
   sugar
¼ teaspoon salt
2 egg yolks
1½ cups cold coffee

½ cup milk
½ teaspoon vanilla
2 egg whites
Cream or whipped cream
(optional)

Combine the gelatin, the ¼ cup of sugar, the salt, and the egg yolks in a heavy saucepan. Gradually stir in the coffee and milk.

Cook over low heat, stirring constantly until the mixture thickens and coats a spoon lightly. Do not boil.

Remove from the heat, cool slightly, then stir in the vanilla. Chill until the mixture thickens slightly.

Beat the egg whites until soft peaks form. Gradually beat in the remaining 2 tablespoons of sugar. Fold in the gelatin mixture.

Rinse individual molds or one large mold with cold water and pour in the mixture. Chill until set.

Unmold and serve plain, or with cream or whipped cream. Serves 4.

WINE JELLY

Sparkling jellies were old-time forerunners of packaged fruit-flavored gelatins.

2 envelopes unflavored
  gelatin
½ cup cold water
1½ cups sugar
2½ cups boiling water

1 cup sweet wine*
2 tablespoons lemon juice
¼ teaspoon cinnamon
1 cup heavy cream

Sprinkle the gelatin over the cold water and let stand until softened.

Add the sugar and boiling water, stirring until the gelatin is completely dissolved. Set aside to cool.

Stir in the wine, lemon juice, and cinnamon. Strain if the lemon juice is not already strained. Pour into 8 wine glasses and refrigerate for several hours, until set.

When ready to serve, float the unwhipped cream on the tops of the jelly. Serves 8.

*Homemade wines, such as grape, cherry, blackberry, elderberry, and dandelion, were used. Some of these may be purchased bottled.

HOLLAND RUSK PUDDING

Zwieback is the German name for Holland rusks.

CRUST
12 pieces zwieback
¼ cup finely chopped walnuts
⅓ cup sugar
½ cup melted butter

CREAM FILLING
3 egg yolks
½ cup sugar

¼ teaspoon salt
2 tablespoons cornstarch
2 cups milk
1 teaspoon vanilla

MERINGUE
3 egg whites
¼ teaspoon cream of tartar
3 tablespoons sugar

To make the crust, roll the zwieback to make fine crumbs, or use a blender. (There should be 1¾ cups.) Remove ¾ cup, combine with the walnuts, and set aside for the topping.

Combine the remaining crumbs with the sugar and melted butter. Press into the bottom of a buttered 8-inch-square baking pan. (Butter the sides too.)

For the filling, beat the egg yolks with the sugar, salt, and cornstarch in the top of a double boiler. Gradually stir in the milk. Set over simmering water and cook, stirring constantly until thickened (about 10 minutes).

Stir about half the hot mixture into the egg yolks, then add to the remaining mixture and cook 3 or 4 minutes longer. Remove from the heat. Cool slightly, then stir in the vanilla. Pour into the crumb-lined pan.

For the meringue, beat the egg whites with the cream of tartar until they begin to stand in soft peaks, then gradually beat in the sugar. Continue beating until stiff and shiny.

Spread over the cream filling, covering to the edges so that no filling is exposed. Sprinkle the remaining crumb mixture over the top.

Bake in a 350° oven for 30 minutes. Cool, then serve. Serves 6.

Two spoonfuls of snow will supply the place of one egg, and be equally good. Small beer or bottled ale will also answer the same purpose. The yelks and whites of eggs should each be well beaten in a separate basin.

—Modern American Cookery
by Miss Prudence Smith (1835)

Note: This excerpt is from the section "Directions for Making Puddings." Egg yolks were spelled "yelks" at that time.

TOASTED MARSHMALLOWS

An airy white gelatin pudding cut into squares, then rolled in macaroon or graham cracker crumbs. It is served with a lemon butter sauce.

1 envelope unflavored gelatin	1 teaspoon vanilla
¼ cup cold water	Macaroon crumbs or
1 cup boiling water	graham cracker crumbs
⅔ cup sugar	Lemon Butter Sauce
3 egg whites	(recipe follows)
¼ teaspoon salt	

Soften the gelatin in the cold water in a large bowl. Add the boiling water and sugar and stir until dissolved.

Place the bowl in a second bowl containing ice cubes and cold water. Add the unbeaten egg whites, salt, and vanilla. Beat with an electric mixer until the mixture thickens and becomes stiff and white.

Turn into a lightly oiled 9-inch-square pan and level. Chill until the mixture sets.

To serve, cut the pudding into 3-inch squares. Roll lightly in the macaroon or graham cracker crumbs, covering well and shaking off excess crumbs. Arrange the "toasted marshmallows" in dessert dishes. Serve with the chilled Lemon Butter Sauce. Serves 9.

Lemon Butter Sauce

3 egg yolks	Juice and grated rind of 1
⅓ cup sugar	lemon
½ cup melted butter	½ cup heavy cream

Beat the egg yolks slightly. Gradually add the sugar and beat until thick and lemon-colored. Gradually beat in the warm, melted butter and the lemon juice and rind.

Whip the cream and fold it into the egg yolk mixture. Chill thoroughly.

ORANGE LOAF PUDDING

1 envelope unflavored gelatin	½ cup sugar
¼ cup cold water	⅛ teaspoon salt

1 cup hot water
2 tablespoons lemon juice
½ cup orange juice
   (unstrained but without seeds)
   Grated rind of 1 orange

1 cup heavy cream
1 cup cut marshmallows
9 ladyfingers
Whipped cream, orange slices,
   maraschino cherries (optional)

Soften the gelatin in the cold water.

Combine the sugar, salt, and hot water in a saucepan. Bring to a boil, stirring until the sugar is dissolved, then simmer over low heat for 10 minutes.

Add the softened gelatin and stir until dissolved. Blend in the lemon juice, orange juice, and orange rind. Chill until slightly thickened and syrupy, then beat until foamy.

Whip the cream until it mounds lightly and fold into the gelatin mixture. Fold in the cut marshmallows.

Line the bottom of an 8½x4½x2½-inch loaf pan with waxed paper, then lightly oil the sides.

Split the ladyfingers and line the bottom of the mold with a row of one-third of the ladyfingers, rounded side down. Cover with half the gelatin mixture. Add a layer of ladyfingers, the remaining gelatin mixture, and top with the remaining ladyfingers. Press into the mixture lightly. Chill until firm.

Unmold the dessert onto an oblong serving platter. Frost with additional whipped cream and decorate with orange slices and maraschino cherries, if desired. Serves 6.

TO CLARIFY ISINGLASS

Dissolve an ounce of isinglass in a cup of boiling water, take off the scum, and drain through a coarse cloth. Jellies, candies and blanc-mange should be done in brass and stirred with silver.

—Miss Beecher's Housekeeper and Healthkeeper
by Catharine E. Beecher (1873)

PEPPERMINT BAVARIAN CREAM

Although Bavarians are often made of custard or fruit puree lightened with whipped cream and set with gelatin, they may consist simply of cream folded into a sweetened and flavored base. Of the latter, none is more popular than that made with crushed peppermint candies, here served with a hot chocolate sauce.

½ cup (4 ounces) crushed
   peppermint candies*
1 package unflavored gelatin
½ teaspoon salt

2 cups milk
1 cup heavy cream
  Hot Chocolate Sauce
  (recipe follows)

Pulverize the candies in a blender. Combine with the gelatin and salt in a heavy saucepan. Gradually stir in the milk.

Cook over low heat, stirring until the gelatin and candies are dissolved. Remove from the heat and chill until slightly thickened and syrupy, then whip until foamy.

Whip the cream until it mounds lightly but is not stiff. Gradually fold into the gelatin mixture.

Pour into a 1-quart mold that has been rinsed with cold water. Cover with lightly oiled waxed paper and chill until firm (at least 2 hours, or overnight if desired).

Unmold and serve with Hot Chocolate Sauce. Serves 6.

Hot Chocolate Sauce

2 1-ounce squares
  unsweetened chocolate
1½ tablespoons butter
1 tablespoon light corn syrup

¼ cup sugar
⅛ teaspoon salt
3 tablespoons heavy cream
¼ teaspoon vanilla

Melt the chocolate with the butter in the top of a double boiler over hot, not simmering, water. Blend in the corn syrup, sugar, and salt.

Add the cream and cook, stirring for about 10 minutes. Cool slightly, then stir in the vanilla.

If not to be served immediately, keep hot over hot water.

*Round, flat peppermint candies with red-and-white stripes

GINGER CREAM

Another version of Bavarian Cream.

1 envelope unflavored gelatin
¼ cup cold water
⅔ cup milk
3 tablespoons sugar
⅛ teaspoon salt
3 egg yolks

2 tablespoons finely diced
   preserved ginger
2 tablespoons ginger syrup
1 cup heavy cream
   Whipped cream and ginger
   slivers (optional)

Sprinkle the gelatin over the cold water and set aside to soften.

Heat the milk with the softened gelatin, sugar, and salt in a heavy saucepan, stirring until bubbles appear around the edge and the sugar is dissolved.

Beat the egg yolks slightly. Slowly stir the hot milk mixture into the eggs. Return to the saucepan and cook over low heat, stirring constantly until the mixture coats a clean metal spoon. (Do not allow the mixture to boil, or it will curdle.) Remove from the heat; strain, then stir in the ginger and ginger syrup. Cool at room temperature, stirring occasionally until the mixture mounds lightly when dropped from a spoon.

Beat the cream until it mounds softly but is not stiff. Fold it into the gelatin mixture. Turn into a 3-cup mold that has been rinsed with cold water. Chill until set (at least 2 hours, or overnight if preferred).

Unmold on a chilled platter. If desired, garnish with additional sweetened whipped cream forced through a pastry tube and topped with slivers of ginger. Serves 6.

CHARLOTTE RUSSE

This dessert, which was popular in the 1800s and remains a favorite in the South, is created by setting Bavarian Cream in the framework of ladyfingers arranged around the sides of a straight-sided mold. Of the many versions, this is one of the simplest.

12 ladyfingers
2 envelopes unflavored
   gelatin
¾ cup sugar

¼ teaspoon salt
3 cups milk
¼ cup white rum or brandy
2 cups heavy cream

Split the ladyfingers and arrange, sugared sides out, around the sides of a 9-inch springform pan.

Combine the gelatin, sugar, and salt in a heavy saucepan. Gradually stir in the milk. Place over low heat, stirring constantly until the gelatin and sugar are dissolved. Remove from the heat.

Chill until slightly thickened and syrupy. Stir in the rum or brandy and beat until fluffy.

Whip the cream until it mounds lightly but is not stiff. Fold it into the gelatin mixture.

Turn into the prepared pan. Cover the top with a lightly oiled sheet of waxed paper. Chill until firm (several hours or overnight).

To unmold, release the spring and carefully remove the sides of the mold. Serves 12.

Measuring cups are now obtainable with spouts and these are especially useful for measuring liquids. Any good cook will enjoy using one.

—The Menu Book of the American Housewife
(1929)

*Fruit desserts are always popular,
and here's one that can be served year-round—
a colorful and refreshing combination
of generally available Fruit in Sour Cream (page 195).*

CHOCOLATE CHARLOTTE RUSSE

4 1-ounce squares
  unsweetened chocolate
¾ cup sugar
⅓ cup milk
6 egg yolks
1½ cups sweet butter (unsalted)
1½ cups sifted confectioners'
  sugar
6 egg whites

⅛ teaspoon salt
1½ teaspoons vanilla
36 ladyfingers

TOPPING
¾ cup heavy cream
  Shaved unsweetened
  chocolate

Melt the chocolate in the top of a double boiler set over hot water. Cool slightly.

Combine the sugar, milk, and egg yolks in a small heavy saucepan. Cook over low heat, stirring constantly until the sugar dissolves and the mixture thickens slightly. (Do not boil.) Cool.

Cream the butter. Gradually blend in ¾ cup of the confectioners' sugar. Add the cooled chocolate and egg yolk mixture; beat well.

Beat the egg whites with the salt until soft peaks form. Gradually beat in the remaining ¾ cup of confectioners' sugar. Continue beating until stiff but not dry. Stir about one-third of the egg whites into the chocolate mixture to lighten it, then fold in the remainder along with the vanilla.

Line the bottom and sides of a 9-inch springform pan with the split ladyfingers, rounded side out. Add one-third of the chocolate mixture, then a layer of ladyfingers. Repeat the layers, ending with ladyfingers.

Cover with a lightly oiled sheet of waxed paper and chill overnight.

To serve, release the spring and remove the sides. Set the dessert on a serving platter.

To make the topping, whip the cream until stiff and spread over the top. Garnish with the shaved chocolate. Serves 12 to 16.

Note: This dessert may be frozen. Thaw in the refrigerator.

SYLLABUB

An old-fashioned sweet dish made with wine and cream. There are many interpretations.

2 egg whites
⅛ teaspoon salt
½ cup sugar
2 cups heavy cream

2 tablespoons sweet sherry
  or brandy (or more to
  taste)

Beat the egg whites with the salt until soft peaks form. Gradually beat in the sugar and whip until stiff and glossy.

Beat the cream until stiff and fold in. Then fold in the sherry or brandy.

Spoon into parfait glasses and serve immediately. Ladyfingers or slices of pound cake make a nice accompaniment. Serves 8.

COUNTRY SYLLABUB

Mix half a pound of white sugar with a pint of fine cider, or of white wine, and grate in a nutmeg. Prepare them in a large bowl, just before milking time. Then let it be taken to the cow, and have about three pints milked into it, stirring it occasionally with a spoon. Let it be eaten before the froth subsides. If you use cider, a little brandy will improve it.

—Directions for Cookery in Its Various Branches
by Miss [Eliza] Leslie, Seventh Edition (1839)

HEAVENLY HASH

Marshmallows were invented in America and sold as confections in the 1800s. By the early 1900s they were also used in desserts. Desserts that combined marshmallows and cream inspired a series of celestial names such as Heavenly Hash, Food for the Gods, Divinity Parfait, and Glorified Rice.

2 cups fresh dark sweet
   cherries, halved and pitted
2 cups diced fresh pineapple
1 cup orange sections
1 cup seedless green grapes
1 cup slivered blanched
   almonds
2 cups marshmallows cut into
   eighths (use wet scissors)

SOUR CREAM SAUCE
2 eggs
2 tablespoons sugar
¼ cup orange juice
2 tablespoons vinegar
1 tablespoon butter
2 cups dairy sour cream
   Fruits and mint for garnish
   (optional)

Combine the cherries, pineapple, and oranges with the grapes and almonds. Add the marshmallows.

To make the sauce, beat the eggs slightly and gradually beat in the sugar until light. Stir in the orange juice and vinegar. Turn into a heavy saucepan and cook, stirring over low heat until the mixture thickens slightly and coats a spoon. Remove from the heat and blend in the butter. Cool, then fold into the sour cream.

Fold the sauce into the fruits and turn into a serving bowl. Cover and chill for at least 24 hours to allow the flavors to blend.

Serve from the bowl, garnished with additional fruits and sprigs of mint if desired. Serves 10 to 12.

DIVINITY PARFAIT

1 cup heavy cream
2 tablespoons confectioners'
   sugar
½ teaspoon vanilla
16 large marshmallows, cut
   into quarters

8 maraschino cherries, cut
   into small pieces
¼ cup broken English walnuts
   Whole maraschino cherries
   for garnish (optional)

Whip the cream until stiff. Fold in the confectioners' sugar and vanilla, then the marshmallows, cherries, and nuts.

Chill for at least 30 minutes. Serve in sherbet glasses, topped with additional cherries if desired. Serves 4.

GLORIFIED RICE

1 cup uncooked rice
4 cups boiling water
1 teaspoon salt
½ cup sugar
1 8-ounce can crushed
   pineapple, well-drained

12 large marshmallows, cut
   into quarters
1 cup heavy cream
   Maraschino cherries for
   garnish (optional)

Cook the rice, covered, in the boiling, salted water until tender (about 14 minutes). Empty into a colander and rinse thoroughly with cold water, then drain well.

Combine the rice with the sugar and drained pineapple, stirring until the sugar is dissolved. Add the cut marshmallows.

Whip the cream until stiff and fold it into the rice mixture. Chill for several hours.

Spoon into sherbet glasses and garnish with maraschino cherries if desired. Serves 10.

PINEAPPLE ICEBOX CAKE

Although many refrigerated desserts can be considered in the "icebox" category, these particular desserts consist of uncooked fillings made with eggs and butter and put into crumb-lined pans. Icebox desserts of this type have remained popular since their introduction in the early 1900s.

1¾ cups (6 ounces) graham
   cracker crumbs
¾ cup (1½ sticks) softened
   butter
2 cups sifted confectioners'
   sugar

3 eggs
2 tablespoons whiskey
1 cup heavy cream
1 8-ounce can crushed
   pineapple, well-drained
1 cup chopped pecans

Sprinkle half the crumbs evenly over the bottom of a 13x9-inch pan. Reserve the remainder.

Cream the butter and sugar with an electric mixer until light and fluffy. Add the eggs, one at a time, and beat until thick and creamy. Blend in the whiskey.

Spread the butter mixture evenly over the crumbs in the pan.

Whip the cream until stiff. Fold in the drained pineapple and pecans. Spread over the butter mixture.

Sprinkle the remaining crumbs over the top and press them in gently with the palm of your hand. Cover and refrigerate for at least 24 hours.

Cut into squares to serve. Serves 12.

ENGLISH TOFFEE

¾ cup vanilla wafer crumbs
½ cup finely chopped toasted
   almonds
 2 1-ounce squares
   unsweetened chocolate
½ cup (1 stick) softened butter
 2 cups sifted confectioners'
   sugar

2 egg yolks
2 egg whites
1 cup heavy cream
1 tablespoon rum
   Maraschino cherries for
   garnish (optional)

Combine the crumbs and toasted almonds. Sprinkle half over the bottom of a 9-inch-square pan. Reserve the remainder.

Melt the chocolate; set aside to cool slightly.

Cream the butter and sugar with an electric mixer until light and fluffy. Add the egg yolks one at a time and beat until thick and creamy. Stir in the melted chocolate.

Beat the egg whites until soft peaks form, not until stiff. Stir (do not fold) into the chocolate mixture. Spread the chocolate mixture over the nut-crumb mixture in the pan.

Sprinkle the remainder of the crumb mixture over the top and pat down lightly. Refrigerate overnight, or freeze for 2 to 3 hours.

To serve, whip the cream until stiff, adding the rum toward the end of the beating. Cut the dessert into 16 squares. For each serving, place one square on a dessert plate, spread with a layer of whipped cream, then place a second square on top and garnish with a topknot of whipped cream. Add a maraschino cherry for garnish if desired. Serves 8.

DELUXE CHEESECAKE

Cheesecakes are at least as old as written history, but no country seems to have created such varied interpretations as has America. Of the vast array of possibilities, the one described here is certainly one of the grandest of them all. It has a sweet pastry crust, a delicately flavored cream cheese filling, and a topping of glazed fresh strawberries.

SWEET PASTRY CRUST
¾ cup sifted all-purpose flour
3 tablespoons sugar
1 teaspoon grated lemon rind
5 tablespoons softened
    butter
1 egg yolk
¼ teaspoon vanilla

CREAM CHEESE FILLING
4 8-ounce packages cream
    cheese
½ teaspoon grated lemon rind
½ teaspoon grated orange
    rind
1½ cups sugar

2 tablespoons all-purpose
    flour
¼ teaspoon salt
4 eggs
1 egg yolk
3 tablespoons heavy cream
¼ teaspoon vanilla

STRAWBERRY GLAZE
1 quart fresh strawberries
½ cup sugar
¼ cup water
4 teaspoons cornstarch
1 teaspoon butter
    Red food coloring

To prepare the crust, combine the flour, sugar, and lemon rind in a mixing bowl. Cut in the butter with a fork or a pastry blender until crumbly. Add the egg yolk and vanilla and stir until the mixture clings together.

Pat the dough firmly onto the bottom of a 9-inch springform pan with the sides removed. Bake in a 400° oven for 10 minutes, or until light brown. Cool. Reduce the heat to 250°.

For the filling, soften the cream cheese at room temperature. Beat until fluffy. Add the lemon and orange rinds.

Combine the sugar, flour, and salt. Gradually blend into the cream cheese, beating until smooth. Beat in the eggs and egg yolk one at a time, then stir in the cream and vanilla.

Butter the sides of the springform pan and attach to the bottom. Pour in the filling.

Bake in a 250° oven for 1¼ to 1½ hours or until set. Turn off the heat, open the oven door, and allow to cool in the oven for 15 minutes. Then set on a rack away from drafts and cool to room temperature. Release the spring and remove the sides of the pan carefully.

For the topping, rinse, drain, and remove the hulls from the strawberries. Crush enough of the softest and least attractive berries to make ½ cup. Set these aside.

Arrange the whole berries, points up, on top of the cooled cheesecake.

Put the crushed berries, sugar, water, and cornstarch into a small saucepan. Cook, stirring until the mixture comes to a boil and is thickened and clear. Remove from the heat and stir in the butter and a few drops of the food coloring. Strain and cool slightly.

Pour the warm syrup over the berries, allowing some to dribble over the sides. Refrigerate the cheesecake until thoroughly chilled. Serves 12.

REFRIGERATOR CHEESECAKE

A simplification of cheesecake, this one is not baked, merely set with gelatin and chilled.

1 envelope unflavored gelatin	1 teaspoon vanilla
½ cup sugar	A 9-inch baked graham
1 cup boiling water	cracker crust (page 147)
2 8-ounce packages cream	
cheese	

Combine the gelatin and sugar in a bowl. Add the boiling water and stir until the gelatin and sugar are completely dissolved.

Soften the cream cheese to room temperature. Beat until light and fluffy. Gradually beat in the hot gelatin mixture and the vanilla, beating just until smooth.

Pour into the baked graham cracker crust. Chill until firm (about 2 hours). Serves 6 to 8.

CHEESECAKE WITH SOUR CREAM TOPPING

ZWIEBACK CRUST
8 pieces zwieback
1 tablespoon sugar
¼ cup melted butter

CREAM CHEESE FILLING
11 ounces cream cheese
½ cup sugar

2 eggs
½ teaspoon vanilla

SOUR CREAM TOPPING
1 cup sour cream
½ cup sugar
½ teaspoon vanilla

To make the crust, break the zwieback into pieces and turn into crumbs in a blender. (There should be 1¼ cups.) Combine with the sugar. Add the butter and work with a fork or your fingers until the crumbs are well moistened.

Press the mixture evenly and firmly onto the bottom and sides of a 9-inch pie plate. Bake at 350° for 10 minutes. Cool.

For the filling, soften the cream cheese at room temperature. Beat until light and fluffy. Beat in the sugar, then the eggs, one at a time. Blend in the vanilla.

Turn into the prepared crust. Bake at 350° for 15 to 20 minutes, or until firm in the center. Remove and cool for 10 minutes on a rack to allow it to settle.

For the topping, combine the sour cream, sugar, and vanilla. Spread evenly over the top of the pie. Return to the oven and bake 5 minutes longer.

Cool to room temperature on a rack and serve, or chill and serve. Serves 6.

II

Baked and Steamed
Puddings

THOUGH THE POPULAR cold puddings and refrigerated desserts were heavily influenced by the traditions of England and France, most of the popular cooked puddings can be called American with justification. Early settlers found flour and refined sugar in short supply. American Indians introduced them to cornmeal as a flour substitute, and their own ingenuity led them to use molasses, honey, and maple syrup in place of sugar. Native wild berries, cranberries, pumpkins, currants, and nuts formed the remaining elements for their cooked puddings.

It is reported that the Indians made a bread with mashed strawberries that is alleged by some to be the origin of Strawberry Shortcake. The recipe for Indian Pudding, which is made with molasses and cornmeal, is a holdover from this period in American history.

As the New England colonies grew more diverse, other puddings were created to respond to more varied tastes. Among the survivors are Blueberry Grunt and Apple Pandowdy. Other favorites, such as cobblers, baked fruit dumplings, and cottage puddings, came later as variations of the earlier successes.

Interesting new innovations of batter puddings are those that produce their own sauces during baking, of which the current favorite seems to be Chocolate Fudge Pudding.

Baked custards and bread puddings were adopted from England, as were the steamed puddings. In the early days, following English tradition, puddings were boiled in cloth bags; today the preferred method is to steam them. A few steamed puddings from Early America have weathered the years, such as Plum Pudding (now often baked) and others that are made with native New England ingredients.

Steamed Puddings

Two methods are used for steaming pudding mixtures. In the first the pudding is placed in a mold and steamed on a rack set over boiling water. A steamer, which contains a rack, or a kettle inserted with a rack (each with a tight-fitting lid) may be used. This method is required for light batters that will steam in 1 hour or less.

Heavy batters, often containing preserved fruits, are steamed considerably longer. In this method the mold is set on a rack and boiling water is added to come halfway up the sides of the mold.

Pudding molds, bowls, coffee cans, etc., are suitable containers for large puddings. Custard cups, coffee cups, or jelly glasses can be used for individual puddings.

Here are some points to keep in mind.

1. The mold (or molds) should be greased well, then filled no more than two-thirds to three-fourths full to allow for the expansion of the batter. (If the batter is very light and spongy, fill only two-thirds full.)

2. The mold should be covered with a lid or aluminum foil tied with a string. This will prevent the condensed steam that collects on the lid of the steamer from dropping onto the pudding.

3. The steamer should be covered throughout the steaming process and the water for either method replenished as it boils away. Once the water is boiling vigorously, the heat may be turned down slightly so that it boils gently.

4. After steaming, the pudding should be removed from the steamer, uncovered, and allowed to stand for several minutes before being turned out. (Large molds should stand for at least 10 minutes.) When cooled slightly, the pudding will not crack.

5. To unmold the pudding, loosen the edges with a spatula and shake gently to be sure that it is coming away from the sides. Place a serving plate over the mold, invert, and remove the mold carefully.

Note: In general, steamed puddings are only lightly sweetened and should be accompanied by a sauce.

CUP CUSTARD

There's nothing so plain nor so satisfying as a simple baked custard.

2 cups milk	¼ teaspoon salt
2 eggs	¼ teaspoon vanilla
2 egg yolks	¼ teaspoon almond extract
4 tablespoons sugar	Freshly grated nutmeg

Heat the milk in a saucepan until small bubbles appear around the edge.

Combine the eggs, egg yolks, sugar, salt, vanilla, and almond extract. Do not beat. Slowly pour the hot milk into the egg mixture, stirring constantly.

Strain into six 5- or 6-ounce custard cups. Grate the nutmeg lightly over the top. Place the cups in a shallow pan and pour 1 inch of hot water into the pan.

Bake in a 325° oven for 40 to 45 minutes, or until a knife inserted to one side of the center comes out clean, not milky-looking. (The centers will set as the custards cool.) Remove the cups from the hot water and cool.

Serve at room temperature or chilled. Serves 6.

BREAD AND BUTTER LOAF PUDDING

Originally developed to use stale bread, bread puddings became so popular that the modern versions are made with the bread that almost never goes stale. The one selected is typical; it is served with an old-fashioned clear lemon sauce flavored with nutmeg.

6 slices white bread (firm, thin sandwich-style)	1 egg yolk
2 tablespoons soft butter	8 tablespoons sugar
¼ cup seedless raisins	½ teaspoon vanilla
2 cups milk	Nutmeg Sauce (recipe
2 eggs	follows)

Spread one side of the bread slices with the soft butter. (Do not trim off the crusts.) Place 2 slices, buttered sides up, in a buttered

9×5×3½-inch loaf pan. Sprinkle with a few of the raisins. Repeat the layers with the remaining bread and raisins.

Heat the milk in a saucepan until bubbles appear around the edge.

Blend the eggs, egg yolk, 6 tablespoons of sugar, and the vanilla; do not beat. Slowly stir in the hot milk. Pour the mixture evenly over the bread through a wire strainer. Sprinkle the remaining 2 tablespoons of sugar evenly over the top.

Place the loaf pan in a pan and pour 1 inch of hot water into the pan. Bake in a 350° oven until the custard is set (45 minutes to 1 hour). Test by inserting a knife between the bread slices near the center. If it comes out clean, not milky-looking, the custard is done.

Cool slightly and serve warm, plain; or cool to room temperature and serve with Nutmeg Sauce. Serves 4 to 6.

Nutmeg Sauce

½ cup sugar	¾ cup water
2 teaspoons cornstarch	2 tablespoons butter
½ teaspoon freshly grated nutmeg	2 teaspoons lemon juice

Combine the sugar, cornstarch, and nutmeg in a saucepan or the top of a double boiler. Gradually stir in the water. Bring to a boil over medium heat, stirring until the mixture thickens and is clear.

Remove from the heat and stir in the butter and lemon juice. Serve immediately, or keep hot by setting the pan in, or over, hot water.

PLAIN BAKED BREAD PUDDING

Pound fine rusked bread;—to half a teacup of it, put a quart of milk, three eggs, three spoonfuls of powder-sugar, three of drawn butter, and half a nutmeg; bake about one hour—eat without sauce.
—The Improved Housewife, or Book of Receipts
by Mrs. A. L. Webster, 1854 Edition (1843)

QUEEN OF PUDDINGS

This is a classic old-time bread pudding with a meringue topping.

3 cups soft bread cubes (crusts removed)	½ cup tart jelly or preserves
4 egg yolks	**MERINGUE TOPPING**
½ cup sugar	4 egg whites
3 cups milk	1 tablespoon lemon juice
3 tablespoons butter	8 tablespoons sugar

Place the bread cubes in a buttered 2-quart baking dish.

Beat the egg yolks slightly; add the sugar and mix lightly.

Heat the milk with the butter until bubbles appear around the edge. Slowly stir into the egg yolk mixture, stirring until the sugar is dissolved. Strain the mixture over the bread cubes in the baking dish.

Set the baking dish in a shallow pan and pour 1 inch of hot water into the pan. Bake in a 350° oven for 45 to 55 minutes, or until a knife inserted near the edge comes out clean.

Dot the hot pudding with the jelly or preserves.

To make the meringue, beat the egg whites until frothy. Add the lemon juice and beat until soft peaks form, then gradually beat in the sugar. Continue beating until the meringue is stiff and glossy. Swirl over the pudding, covering completely and sealing to the edges of the baking dish.

Return the pudding to the 350° oven (in the pan of water) and bake for 10 to 15 minutes, or until lightly browned.

Serve slightly warm or cooled to room temperature. Spoon into serving dishes (the custard is soft, not firm). Serves 6 to 8.

INDIAN PUDDING

Our ancestors referred to this pudding as Indian Meal Pudding. The chief ingredient is cornmeal, or Indian meal, which had been used by Indian tribes long before the first white settlers incorporated it into their diets. In New England tradition, part of the milk is stirred in during baking, which produces a characteristic creamy center beneath a reddish brown crust.

6 cups milk	1½ teaspoons ginger
7 tablespoons yellow cornmeal	2 tablespoons butter
1 cup molasses	Milk, cream, or vanilla ice cream
1 teaspoon salt	

Gradually stir 1 cup of milk into the cornmeal, then blend in the molasses, salt, and ginger.

Scald 3 cups of milk with the butter, then gradually stir into the cornmeal mixture.

Pour into a buttered 1½-quart baking dish and bake at 325° for 1 hour. Stir in the remaining 2 cups of milk and continue baking 2 hours longer.

Serve warm with milk, cream, or ice cream. Serves 8.

When you make batter-puddings, first mix the flour well with a little milk, then put in the ingredients by degrees, and it will be quite smooth; but for a plain batter-pudding, the best way is to strain it through a coarse hair-sieve, that it may neither have lumps nor treadles of the eggs; and for all other puddings strain the eggs when you beat them. Bread and custard-puddings for baking require time and a moderate oven to raise them; batter and rice pudding a quick oven.

—Modern American Cookery
by Miss Prudence Smith (1835)

APPLE BROWN BETTY

A favorite dessert of many. When rhubarb replaces the apples, it is known as Blushing Betty.

3 cups soft bread cubes	½ cup water
7 tablespoons melted butter	Grated rind of 1 lemon
3 cups sliced tart apples	3 tablespoons lemon juice
1 cup sugar	Light cream or vanilla ice
1 teaspoon cinnamon	cream
½ teaspoon nutmeg	

Place half the bread cubes in a buttered shallow 1½-quart baking dish. Mix the remaining cubes with 2 tablespoons of melted butter; set aside.

Spread the apple slices over the bread cubes in the baking dish. Combine the sugar, cinnamon, nutmeg, water, lemon rind and juice, and the remaining 5 tablespoons of melted butter. Stir until the sugar is dissolved. Pour this mixture over the apples and top with the reserved buttered bread cubes.

Bake in a 375° oven for 30 to 40 minutes, or until the apples are tender and the bread is well browned. (Check toward the end of baking; if the bread is browning too quickly, cover lightly with foil.)

Serve warm or cold with light cream or ice cream. Serves 6.

OZARK PUDDING

Originating in Missouri, this firm apple pudding crossed the border to become a national favorite.

1 egg	½ cup chopped tart apples
½ cup sugar	½ cup chopped pecans
2 tablespoons flour	1 teaspoon vanilla
1¼ teaspoons baking powder	Vanilla ice cream
⅛ teaspoon salt	

Beat the egg and sugar together until light. Sift the flour, baking powder, and salt together; stir into the egg mixture.

Add the apples, pecans, and vanilla; mix well.

Turn into a buttered 8-inch pie plate and bake at 350° for 35 minutes.

Cut into wedges and serve warm with ice cream. Serves 6.

PLUM SKILLET CAKE

Upside-down cakes, as they are known today, first appeared in cookbooks at the turn of the twentieth century. Pineapple is the best known, but other fruits are used with equal success.

7 tablespoons butter
½ cup light brown sugar
   (packed)
1 pound prune plums or
   small blue plums

CAKE BATTER
2 egg yolks
1 teaspoon lemon extract

1 cup sugar
5 tablespoons hot water
1 cup sifted cake flour
1 teaspoon baking powder
½ teaspoon salt
3 egg whites
   Whipped cream for garnish
   (optional)

Melt the butter slowly in a 10-inch heavy skillet or a 9-inch-square baking pan. Remove from the heat and sprinkle the brown sugar evenly in the skillet or pan.

Split the plums, removing the pits. Arrange them cut side down in the skillet. Set aside.

To make the cake batter, beat the egg yolks with the lemon extract until thick and lemon-colored. Gradually beat in the sugar, then the hot water.

Sift together the flour, baking powder, and salt. Blend into the egg yolk mixture all at one time.

Beat the egg whites until stiff, then fold in.

Pour this batter over the plums in the skillet or pan. Bake at 350° for 40 to 45 minutes, or until the cake tests done with a pick.

Remove the cake from the oven and immediately turn the skillet or pan upside down on a serving platter. Let stand for a few minutes until all the sugar mixture adheres to the cake, then remove the skillet or pan.

Serve warm, plain, or top with whipped cream. Serves 8.

PRUNE WHIP

This old-time favorite is a type of soufflé made with egg whites.

1 cup finely chopped cooked prunes*	1 tablespoon lemon juice
⅓ cup sugar	⅓ cup finely chopped walnuts
3 egg whites	1 teaspoon vanilla
¼ teaspoon salt	Pouring Custard (recipe follows)

Combine the cooled prunes with the sugar.

Beat the egg whites until foamy. Add the salt and lemon juice and beat until soft peaks form. Gradually beat in the sugared prunes, then continue beating until very thick and glossy. Fold in the walnuts and vanilla.

Turn into a buttered and lightly sugared 1½-quart soufflé dish or casserole. Set in a pan of hot water to come up 1 inch on the sides.

Bake in a 375° oven until lightly browned and firm (about 20 to 25 minutes). Test in the center with a wooden pick; it should come out clean.

Serve at once with the chilled Pouring Custard. Serves 4 to 6.

*Prunes labeled "ready to eat" may be used without cooking.

Pouring Custard

1½ cups milk	¼ cup sugar
3 egg yolks	½ teaspoon vanilla

Heat the milk in a heavy saucepan until bubbles appear around the edge.

Beat the egg yolks slightly. Stir in the sugar; do not beat. Gradually stir the hot milk into the eggs and return to the saucepan.

Cook over low heat, stirring constantly until the mixture thickens slightly and will coat a clean metal spoon with a thin, creamy film.

Cool slightly, then stir in the vanilla. Cover and cool to room temperature. Refrigerate until thoroughly chilled.

RHUBARB SPONGE CUSTARD

During the baking the pudding batter separates into layers of sponge and custard. Puddings of this type are often known as cake puddings.

1 cup sugar
2 tablespoons flour
1 tablespoon softened butter
2 egg yolks
1 cup milk

1 cup diced fresh rhubarb
2 egg whites
⅛ teaspoon salt
Whipped cream (optional)

Combine the sugar and flour in a mixing bowl. Cut in the butter with a pastry blender until fine.

Beat the egg yolks slightly and stir in the milk. Stir into the sugar mixture along with the rhubarb.

Beat the egg whites with the salt until stiff. Fold into the rhubarb mixture.

Turn into a 1-quart shallow baking dish and set in a pan containing 1 inch of hot water. Bake at 375° for 35 to 40 minutes, or until the pudding is set and the top is golden brown.

Serve slightly warm or cool, plain or with whipped cream. Serves 6.

VANITY FAIR

Rich and chewy. Best served warm with whipped cream.

1 cup dates
1 cup broken pecans
1 tablespoon fine dry or soft
  bread crumbs

1 cup sugar
1 teaspoon baking powder
3 eggs
Whipped cream

Snip the dates into small pieces with wet scissors. Combine with the pecans and bread crumbs. Combine the sugar and baking powder; stir into the date mixture.

Beat the eggs well, then blend in.

Turn into a buttered 8-inch-square baking pan. Bake at 350° for 30 minutes.

Cut into squares and serve warm with whipped cream. Serves 6.

STRAWBERRY SHORTCAKES

This old-fashioned shortcake is made with a biscuit dough rather than
with sponge cake. It is served topped with juicy sweetened
strawberries and pouring cream.

TOPPING
1 pint fresh strawberries
½ cup sugar
Softened butter
Heavy cream

BISCUIT DOUGH
1½ cups sifted all-purpose flour
2 teaspoons baking powder
¾ teaspoon salt
2 teaspoons sugar
4 tablespoons softened
butter
½ cup milk (about)

Prepare the strawberries before making the biscuit dough.
Rinse, dry, and remove the hulls. Slice the berries into a bowl; add the
½ cup of sugar and mix gently. Let stand, stirring occasionally until a
juice forms and the sugar is dissolved (20 to 30 minutes). (If allowed to
stand for several hours the berries will soften and give up an excess
amount of juice.)

To prepare the biscuit dough, sift the flour with the baking
powder, salt, and sugar 3 times. Cut in the butter with a pastry
blender. Add the milk, saving about 1 tablespoon. Stir with a fork
until all the flour is dampened, adding a few drops more milk if the
mixture seems dry. Then stir vigorously until the mixture forms a
very soft dough and collects into a ball.

Turn out on a lightly floured board and knead gently for 30
seconds. Pat or roll ½ inch thick. Cut into 4 circles with a 2½-inch
floured biscuit cutter.

Place the biscuits on an ungreased baking sheet and bake in a
450° oven for 12 to 14 minutes, or until golden.

Separate the hot biscuits into halves and spread the insides
generously with the soft butter. Re-form on dessert plates, filling and
topping with the berries and juices. Serve immediately, with a pitcher
of heavy cream. Serves 4.

COTTAGE PUDDING

Cottage pudding is a simple batter, usually made with one egg, which is baked in one layer in a square pan, cut, and served warm with a hot sauce. For the sauce, lemon is the traditional favorite.

1½ cups sifted all-purpose flour	1 egg
¾ cup sugar	½ cup milk
3 teaspoons baking powder	1 teaspoon vanilla
½ teaspoon salt	Lemon Sauce (recipe
¼ cup vegetable shortening	follows)

Sift the flour, sugar, baking powder, and salt together into a mixing bowl. Cut in the shortening until the mixture resembles coarse meal.

Beat the egg well; combine with the milk and vanilla. Add to the flour mixture. Beat with a rotary beater or a spoon until smooth.

Turn into a well-greased 8-inch-square baking pan. Spread evenly and bake at 375° for 25 to 30 minutes, or until the cake tests done with a pick.

Cut into squares and serve warm with hot Lemon Sauce. Serves 9.

Lemon Sauce

1 cup sugar	1 tablespoon butter
1 tablespoon cornstarch	1½ tablespoons lemon juice
1 cup water	

Combine the sugar and cornstarch in a saucepan. Gradually stir in the water. Cook, stirring over medium heat until the sauce is thickened and clear (about 3 minutes).

Remove from the heat and stir in the butter and lemon juice.

If not to be served immediately, keep hot by setting the pan in a bowl of hot water.

CRANBERRY PUDDING

Another cottage pudding with an outrageously rich butter sauce.

2 cups sifted all-purpose
   flour
1 cup sugar
2 teaspoons baking powder
½ teaspoon salt

⅓ cup vegetable shortening
1 cup milk
2 cups whole raw cranberries
   Creamy Butter Sauce
   (recipe follows)

Sift the flour, sugar, baking powder, and salt together into a mixing bowl. Cut in the shortening with a pastry blender to fine crumbs. Stir in the milk, then the cranberries.

Pour into a greased and floured 9-inch-square baking pan. Bake at 350° for 40 to 45 minutes, or until the cake tests done with a pick inserted in the center.

Cut into squares and serve warm with Creamy Butter Sauce. Serves 9.

Creamy Butter Sauce

1 cup (½ pound) butter
2 cups sugar

1½ cups heavy cream

Combine the butter, sugar, and cream in the top of a double boiler. Bring to a boil, stirring, then set over simmering water and continue cooking until thickened (about 10 minutes). Serve hot.

PEACH COBBLER

A cobbler is a biscuit dough baked either above or beneath a layer of sweetened fruit. The name comes from the Early American expression "cobble up," meaning "to put together quickly."

3 cups sliced fresh peaches
¼ cup sugar
½ teaspoon cinnamon

BISCUIT DOUGH
1 cup sifted all-purpose flour
1 teaspoon baking powder
½ teaspoon salt

1 tablespoon butter
⅓ cup milk

SYRUP
¾ cup sugar
½ cup water
3 tablespoons butter

Arrange the peaches in a buttered shallow 10x6x2-inch or 8-inch-square baking pan. Combine the ¼ cup of sugar with the cinnamon and sprinkle evenly over the top.

To make the biscuit dough, sift the flour with the baking powder and salt. Cut in the butter until the mixture looks like coarse crumbs. Add the milk, stirring to form a soft dough.

Knead the dough a few times, then roll out on a lightly floured board to fit over the peaches. (It is not necessary to cover them completely.) Place on top and cut 4 or 5 slits in the dough to allow the steam to escape.

Bake in a 425° oven for 20 minutes.

Meanwhile, prepare the syrup by combining the sugar, water, and butter in a saucepan. Bring to a boil, stirring until the sugar is dissolved. Boil for 5 minutes without stirring.

Pour the hot syrup over the biscuit dough and continue baking at 425° 10 minutes longer, or until the top is golden.

Serve slightly warm, with cream if desired. Serves 6.

TO TEST THE HEAT OF AN OVEN

Put a spoon of flour on an old dish and set in the oven. If it browns in 60 seconds the heat is right for bread. If it browns in less time, the heat must be lessened. But if it is not browned, the oven is not hot enough. The oft-repeated rule to hold the hand in the oven long enough to count so-and-so is no accurate test, on account of the varying ability of different persons to bear heat. If stoves had a thermometer attachment for the oven door, by which the degree of heat could be seen at all times, the invention would be of incalculable benefit.

—Mrs. Owens' Cook Book and Useful Household Hints
by Frances E. Owens, 1888 Revised Edition (1884)

PEACH KUCHEN

"Kuchen" is a German word meaning "cake." It can be a yeast-raised or baking powder leavened cake, or even a rich, thick pastry filled with fruit. This Dutch cake is of the baking powder type and is easy to make. Other fresh fruits may be used.

1½ cups sifted all-purpose flour	FRUIT TOPPING
3 teaspoons baking powder	5–6 (1½ pounds) ripe peaches
½ teaspoon salt	Lemon juice
¾ cup sugar	½ cup sugar
¼ cup vegetable shortening	1 tablespoon flour
1 egg	¾ teaspoon cinnamon
½ cup milk	2 tablespoons butter
1 teaspoon vanilla	

Sift together the flour, baking powder, salt, and sugar into a mixing bowl. Cut in the shortening with a pastry blender until it resembles coarse meal.

Beat the egg well. Combine with the milk and vanilla. Add to the flour mixture and stir just until well blended.

Pour into a greased 9-inch-square baking pan.

For the topping, peel the peaches, slice into thick wedges, and dip them into water containing a little lemon juice. Drain them and lay them in rows over the thick batter.

Combine the sugar, flour, and cinnamon. Sprinkle over the peaches as evenly as possible. Dot with the butter. Bake in a 375° oven for 40 to 45 minutes, or until the batter puffs up around the peaches and is golden.

Serve warm or cooled, plain or with whipped cream. Serves 9.

Note: This kuchen may be reheated. It retains its fresh quality for a day or two.

BAKED APPLE DUMPLINGS

An old-time recipe for apples wrapped in pastry and baked with syrup. The pastry here contains lard, the fat that was originally used, still preferred by many dumpling makers today.

PASTRY
2 cups sifted all-purpose
flour
2 teaspoons baking powder
1 teaspoon salt
⅔ cup lard
¼–⅓ cup milk

APPLES
6 medium-size tart red
apples*
½ cup sugar

1 teaspoon cinnamon
1 tablespoon butter

SYRUP
2 cups water
Apple peelings
¾ cup sugar
⅓ cup butter
1 tablespoon lemon juice
1 teaspoon grated lemon rind
¼ teaspoon cinnamon

To make the pastry, sift the flour, baking powder, and salt together. Cut in the lard with a pastry blender until fine crumbs are formed. Add ¼ cup of milk, stirring until the mixture holds together. (If necessary, add the remainder of the milk.)

Roll out on a lightly floured board into a 12x18-inch rectangle. Cut into six 6-inch squares.

Peel and core the apples, reserving the skins for the syrup. Place an apple in the center of each pastry square. Combine the ½ cup of sugar with the cinnamon and fill the centers of the apples. Dot each with bits of the butter.

Moisten the edges of the pastry; bring up over the apples, pinching the edges together to seal. Prick each twice with a fork.

Arrange the dumplings in a buttered 12x8x2-inch baking pan. Refrigerate for 30 minutes before baking. (This creates a liquid inside the dumplings.)

Bake in a 425° oven for 15 minutes.

Just before the apples are placed in the oven, prepare the syrup. Bring the water to a boil in a small saucepan. Add the apple peelings, cover, and simmer for 20 minutes. Strain to remove the peelings, then stir in the sugar, butter, lemon juice and rind, and cinnamon. Simmer, stirring until the sugar is dissolved.

When the apples have baked for 15 minutes, pour the hot syrup over the tops, reduce the heat to 350°, and bake 30 to 40 minutes longer, or until the pastry is golden brown and the apples are tender. Baste occasionally with the syrup during baking.

Serve hot with some of the syrup from the pan and with milk or light cream if desired.

*Cortland, Rome Beauty, and McIntosh are varieties that hold their shape during baking.

CARAMEL DUMPLINGS

These dumplings are baked with a sauce in individual cups, then unmolded.

CARAMEL SAUCE	DUMPLINGS
⅔ cup sugar	¾ cup sifted all-purpose flour
¾ cup boiling water	2 tablespoons sugar
1 tablespoon butter	1 teaspoon baking powder
½ teaspoon vanilla	¼ teaspoon salt
	2 tablespoons lard
	¼ cup chopped pecans
	¼ cup milk

To make the sauce, place ⅓ cup of sugar in a small, heavy skillet. Cook, stirring until the sugar is melted and golden brown. Stir in the boiling water, the remaining ⅓ cup of sugar, and the butter. Bring to a boil again, stirring to dissolve the sugar. Boil for 2 minutes. Remove from the heat and stir in the vanilla. Pour into 4 greased custard cups.

For the dumplings, sift the flour, sugar, baking powder, and salt together into a bowl. Cut in the lard with a pastry blender until fine. Add the pecans. Stir in the milk, mixing only enough to dampen all the flour.

Drop the dough by spoonfuls over the hot syrup in the custard cups. Bake in a 400° oven for 20 minutes, or until the tops are brown.

Remove from the oven and loosen the edges, then invert the dumplings in the cups in individual serving dishes. Let stand for 3 minutes before removing the cups.

Serve plain or with whipped cream. Serves 4.

APPLE PANDOWDY

Apple Pandowdy is a cross between a pudding and a deep-dish apple pie. In early New England it was considered a breakfast dish to be served with milk or cream. The name comes from the final step in baking, when the crust is broken up and pushed down into the apples, a process referred to as "dowdy." Pandowdy is the forerunner of the cobbler of today.

¾ cup brown sugar (packed)
¼ cup all-purpose flour
¼ teaspoon salt
1 cup water
2 teaspoons vinegar
¼ cup molasses
4–5 cups (1½ pounds) cooking
  apples, sliced into eighths
½ teaspoon cinnamon

⅛ teaspoon nutmeg
2 tablespoons butter

BISCUIT BATTER
1 cup sifted all-purpose flour
2 teaspoons baking powder
¾ teaspoon salt
3 tablespoons butter
¾ cup milk

Combine the brown sugar, flour, and salt in a saucepan. Gradually stir in the water, vinegar, and molasses. Cook, stirring over medium heat until the mixture is smooth and thickened. Remove from the heat and set aside.

Arrange the sliced apples in a well-greased 12x8x2-inch baking dish. Cover them with the sauce, sprinkle with the cinnamon and nutmeg, and dot with the butter.

To make the biscuit batter, sift the flour, baking powder, and salt into a mixing bowl. Cut in the butter with a pastry blender until it is the size of peas. Add the milk and stir until all parts are dampened. The mixture should remain somewhat lumpy.

Drop the mixture by spoonfuls over the apples (it will not cover them completely). Bake at 375° for 30 minutes. Then break through the biscuit topping with a fork and work it down among the apples. Continue baking for 10 minutes. Serve warm, with cream if desired. Serves 6 to 8.

PAN DOWDY

Put apples pared and sliced into a large pan, and put in an abundance of molasses or sugar, and some spice if the apples have little flavor; not otherwise. Cover with bread-dough, rolled thin, or a potato pie-crust. Bake a long time, and then break the crust into the fruit in small pieces. Children are very fond of this, especially if well sweetened and baked a long time.

—Miss Beecher's Housekeeper and Healthkeeper
by Catharine E. Beecher (1873)

RAISIN PUDDING

An old-time favorite also known as Brown Sugar Pudding.

1 cup sifted all-purpose flour	**BROWN SUGAR SYRUP**
½ cup sugar	1 cup dark brown sugar
2 teaspoons baking powder	(packed)
¼ teaspoon salt	2 cups water
1 teaspoon cinnamon	2 tablespoons butter
½ cup milk	
½ cup raisins	

Sift the flour, sugar, baking powder, salt, and cinnamon together into a mixing bowl. Add the milk and raisins, mixing only enough to dampen the flour.

Turn into an 8-inch-square greased baking pan.

To make the syrup, combine the brown sugar, water, and butter in a saucepan. Bring to a boil, stirring to dissolve the sugar; boil for 5 minutes without stirring.

Pour the hot syrup in a thin stream over the batter. (Do not stir in.) Bake in a 350° oven for 25 to 30 minutes, or until firm.

Cut the pudding into squares, then spoon out and top with the sauce. Serve warm or cold. Serves 6.

Note: If served cold, the sauce becomes quite thick and may be served additionally with thin cream or whipped cream.

CHOCOLATE FUDGE PUDDING

This chocolate pudding and similar ones are known by several names, including Baked Devil's Float, Chocolate Upside-Down Cake, and Brownie Pudding. During the baking the pudding separates to form a sauce on the bottom, cake on the top.

1 cup sifted all-purpose flour	2 tablespoons melted butter
2 teaspoons baking powder	1 teaspoon vanilla
½ teaspoon salt	½ cup chopped pecans
⅔ cup sugar	1 cup brown sugar (packed)
6 tablespoons cocoa	1½ cups boiling water
½ cup milk	

Sift the flour, baking powder, salt, sugar, and 2 tablespoons of cocoa together into a mixing bowl. Add the milk.

Stir in the melted butter and vanilla, mixing only until well blended. Stir in the pecans.

Turn into a greased, shallow 1½-quart baking dish.

Combine the brown sugar with the remaining 4 tablespoons of cocoa. Press with the back of a spoon to break up any sugar lumps. Sprinkle over the mixture in the baking dish. Pour the boiling water over the top. Do not stir in.

Bake at 350° for 40 to 45 minutes. Serve warm or cold. Spoon out a portion of the cake and cover with the sauce. Serves 8.

Note: If served cold, the sauce becomes quite thick and may be served with the addition of whipped cream or thin cream.

WHIPPED CREAM

I have been assured by those who have made the experiment, that excellent whipped cream can be produced and very quickly, by the use of our incomparable Dover Egg-beater. I have never tried this, but my pupils may, if they have not a syllabub-churn.

Put a pint of rich sweet cream in a pail or other wide mouthed vessel with straight sides, and set in ice while you whip or churn it.

As the frothing cream rises to the top, remove it carefully with a spoon and lay it in a perfectly clean and cold colander, or on a hair sieve, set over a bowl. If any cream drips from it return to the vessel in which it is whipped to be beaten over again. When no more froth rises, whip a tablespoonful of powdered sugar into the white syllabub in the colander, and it is ready for use.

—Cookery for Beginners
by Marion Harland (1884)

FRUIT PUDDING

Another pudding that makes its own sauce during baking.

¼ cup butter
1½ cups sugar
  1 cup sifted all-purpose flour
  2 teaspoons baking powder
¼ teaspoon salt
½ cup milk

½ teaspoon vanilla
2 cups pitted fresh cherries,
  berries, or chopped
  peaches
1 cup boiling water

Cream the butter until soft. Gradually add ½ cup of sugar and beat until fluffy.

Sift the flour, baking powder, and salt together. Add alternately to the creamed mixture with the milk and vanilla. Beat until smooth.

Turn into an 8-inch-square baking pan (or similar size pan). Spoon the fruit over the top and sprinkle it with the cup of sugar. Pour the boiling water over the top. Do not stir in.

Bake in a 350° oven for 40 to 45 minutes, or until the pudding begins to shrink from the sides of the pan and the top is golden brown. During the baking the fruit and juice will go to the bottom and a cakelike layer will form on top.

Serve warm, cut into squares with the fruit and syrup spooned over the top. Serves 6.

SAILOR'S DUFF

Duff is an English word for dough, referring to heavy pudding batters that were steamed rather than baked.

  1 egg
  2 tablespoons sugar
½ cup molasses
  3 tablespoons melted butter
1½ cups sifted all-purpose
  flour

1 teaspoon soda
¼ teaspoon salt
½ cup boiling water
  Sailor's Duff Sauce (recipe
  follows)

Beat the egg lightly. Gradually beat in the sugar, molasses, and melted butter.

Sift the flour, soda, and salt together. Stir into the molasses mixture, then stir in the boiling water.

Pour into a greased 1-quart mold; cover tightly. Place on a rack in the bottom of a large kettle or steamer. Add boiling water to come halfway up the mold. Cover and steam for 1½ hours.

Turn out and serve hot with Sailor's Duff Sauce. Serves 6 to 8.

Sailor's Duff Sauce

2 egg yolks	1 teaspoon vanilla extract
1 cup sifted confectioners' sugar	1 cup heavy cream

Beat the egg yolks slightly. Gradually stir in the confectioners' sugar, then the vanilla.

Just before serving, whip the cream lightly so that it can still be poured. Fold into the egg yolk mixture.

FOAM SAUCE

1 cupful of sugar; 1-1/2 table-spoonful of butter; 1 egg; 3 table-spoonfuls of boiling water. Rub the butter and sugar to a cream, and add the yolk of the egg. Place the bowl in a basin of hot water, and add the boiling water by the spoonful, stirring well; and if the sugar does not dissolve readily, keep the bowl in a hot place until all is smooth, stirring continuously. The sauce should be a rich, yellow syrup when finished. Turn it into the serving bowl, and place on top the beaten white of the egg, which must be stirred into the sauce after the latter is on the table.

—Butterick's "Correct Cookery"
(1900)

STRAWBERRY ROLL

This roll is a departure from an old-time dessert called Roly-poly, in which sweetened fruit was rolled up in pastry, then baked in syrup. Here the roll is sliced before baking.

SYRUP
½ cup sugar
2 tablespoons butter
1½ cups water
1 teaspoon vanilla

PASTRY
2 cups sifted all-purpose flour
3 teaspoons baking powder
1 teaspoon salt

2 tablespoons sugar
5 tablespoons vegetable shortening
1 egg
Milk
1 tablespoon soft butter

STRAWBERRY FILLING
4 cups sliced strawberries
½ cup sugar
1 tablespoon melted butter

To make the syrup, combine the sugar, butter, and water in a saucepan. Bring to a boil, then simmer for 5 minutes. Remove from the heat and stir in the vanilla. Pour into a 10x6x2-inch baking pan.

To make the pastry, sift the flour, baking powder, salt, and sugar together into a bowl. Cut in the shortening with a pastry blender until fine. Beat the egg slightly in a measuring cup and add enough milk to make ⅔ cup liquid. Add to the dry ingredients, stirring with a fork to make a soft dough.

Knead lightly, then roll out into a 12x8-inch rectangle. Spread with the soft butter.

To make the filling, rinse and dry the strawberries and remove the hulls. Slice to make 4 cups. Cover the pastry to within ½ inch of the edge with 3 cups of the strawberries and sprinkle them with the sugar. Roll up from the long side as for a jelly roll; pinch the edge into the dough to seal, moistening if necessary.

With a very sharp knife, slice the roll across into 9 slices.

Place the rolls, cut side down, in the syrup. Spread them with the tablespoon of melted butter. Place the remaining cup of strawberries in the syrup around the rolls.

Bake in a 425° oven for 30 to 35 minutes.

Serve warm with some of the syrup from the pan spooned over each roll, and with whipped cream or plain cream if desired. Serves 9.

*A dessert that is as good to look at
as to eat is tart-sweet Glazed Oranges (page 196).*

BLUEBERRY GRUNT

To make a Grunt, a soft biscuit dough is dropped into berries simmering in a skillet or a saucepan. Before stoves were invented, the pudding was cooked in a kettle hung on a crane over an open fire. As the fruit cooked, it bubbled up and made gurgling (or grunting) noises.

2 cups blueberries	**DUMPLINGS**
¾ cup sugar	1 cup sifted all-purpose flour
1 tablespoon lemon juice	¼ cup sugar
Grated rind of 1 lemon	2 teaspoons baking powder
¼ teaspoon cinnamon	½ teaspoon salt
¼ teaspoon salt	3 tablespoons soft shortening
1½ cups water	⅓–½ cup milk

Combine the blueberries, sugar, lemon juice and rind, cinnamon, salt, and water in a heavy 4-quart saucepan. Bring to a boil, then simmer until the berries just begin to render their juices (about 5 minutes). Remove from the heat and set aside.

To prepare the dumplings, sift the flour, sugar, baking powder, and salt together into a bowl. Cut in the shortening with a pastry blender until the mixture resembles fine crumbs. Add enough milk to make a soft, sticky dough, stirring only enough to dampen the flour.

Reheat the berries to a simmer. Drop the dough from a greased tablespoon over the top, forming 6 dumplings. Cook uncovered for 10 minutes, adjusting the heat so that the sauce bubbles slightly; then cover tightly and cook 10 minutes longer. (Do not lift the lid during this period.)

Spoon the dumplings into shallow dessert bowls and pour the blueberry sauce over the top. Serve warm, plain or with heavy cream. Serves 6.

PLUM PUDDING

This traditional Christmas favorite is not actually made with plums but with raisins and other fruit. Of English origin, the early puddings were made with suet. This one replaces the suet with butter. It is served with Brandy Sauce.

¾ cup (4 ounces) seedless
    raisins
¾ cup (4 ounces) currants
¾ cup (4 ounces) finely cut
    citron
¾ cup (4 ounces) finely cut
    candied orange and lemon
    peel
1 cup sugar
½ cup butter
½ cup water

½ cup brandy
1 teaspoon cinnamon
½ teaspoon soda
2 eggs
2 cups sifted all-purpose
    flour
2 teaspoons baking powder
½ teaspoon salt
    Brandy Sauce (recipe
    follows)

Combine the raisins, currants, citron, and candied peels with the sugar in a saucepan. Add the butter, water, brandy, cinnamon, and soda. Bring to a boil, stirring, then turn the heat to low and simmer for 10 minutes. Cool.

Beat the eggs until foamy, then stir into the fruit mixture. Sift the flour, baking powder, and salt together; blend in.

Turn the mixture into two buttered and floured 1-quart pudding molds. Cover tightly and set the molds on a rack in a deep kettle or steamer. Pour boiling water around the molds to a depth half their height. Cover and steam the puddings for 3 hours, adding more boiling water as needed to maintain the required level.

Unmold the puddings. Serve one of them hot with the Brandy Sauce. Serves 8.

Cool the remaining pudding, wrap in foil, and refrigerate. It will keep well for weeks. When ready to serve, re-steam in the original mold for 30 minutes, or until hot.

Brandy Sauce

½ cup sugar
½ cup butter
1 cup water
1 stick cinnamon

4 teaspoons cornstarch
1 tablespoon water
½ cup brandy

Combine the sugar, butter, and water with the whole cinnamon stick in a saucepan. Bring to a boil, cover, and turn the heat to low. Simmer for 15 minutes.

Dissolve the cornstarch in the tablespoon of water. Stir into the cinnamon mixture. Cook until clear (about 3 minutes). Remove from the heat and discard the cinnamon stick. Stir in the brandy and allow to cool. Serve at room temperature.

Note: This recipe provides enough sauce for one Plum Pudding.

ROSE BRANDY
(For Cakes and Puddings)

Gather the leaves of roses while the dew is on them, and as soon as they open, put them into a wide-mouthed bottle, and when the bottle is full, pour in the best of fourth proof French brandy.

It will be fit for use in three or four weeks, and may be frequently replenished. It is sometimes considered preferable to wine as a flavoring to pastries and pudding sauces.

—The White House Cook Book
by Mrs. F. L. Gillette and Hugo Ziemann, 1890 Edition (1887)

STEAMED CRANBERRY PUDDING

1½ cups cranberries	2 teaspoons soda
1 egg	⅓ cup hot water
3 tablespoons sugar	1½ cups sifted all-purpose flour
½ teaspoon salt	Hot Creamy Sauce (recipe
½ cup molasses	follows)

Split each cranberry once, then rinse in a colander under cold running water to remove as many seeds as possible. Set aside to drain well.

Beat the egg with the sugar and salt. Stir in the molasses. Dissolve the soda in the hot water and stir in.

Stir in the cranberries and flour.

Turn into a well-greased 1-quart mold; cover. Place on a rack in the bottom of a large kettle or steamer. Add boiling water to come halfway up the mold. Cover and steam for 1½ hours.

Unmold and serve hot with Hot Creamy Sauce.

Hot Creamy Sauce

½ cup butter	½ cup heavy cream
1 cup sugar	1 teaspoon vanilla

Melt the butter in the top of a double boiler. Stir in the sugar and cream. Bring to a boil, stirring until the sugar melts. Set over hot water until time to serve, then stir in the vanilla.

STEAMED SNOWBALL PUDDING

Served with sweetened strawberries, these white puddings are sometimes called Steamed Strawberry Shortcake.

6 tablespoons vegetable shortening	½ teaspoon salt
1 cup sugar	½ cup milk
½ teaspoon almond extract	3 egg whites
1½ cups sifted cake flour	Sweetened sliced strawberries
1½ teaspoons baking powder	

Cream the shortening and ⅔ cup of sugar. Blend in the almond extract.

Sift together the flour, baking powder, and salt. Add to the creamed mixture alternately with the milk.

Beat the egg whites until soft peaks form, then gradually beat in the remaining ⅓ cup of sugar. Continue beating until stiff and glossy. Fold into the batter.

Turn into 7 or 8 well-greased custard cups or coffee cups. Cover with waxed paper, then foil, and tie with a string.

Place on a rack in a steamer or a large kettle containing 1 inch of boiling water; cover and steam for 30 minutes.

Unmold and serve warm with the strawberries. Serves 7 or 8.

STEAMED CHOCOLATE PUDDING

When steamed, this pudding is similar to a rich chocolate cake.

⅓ cup softened butter	1½ cups sifted all-purpose
1 cup sugar	flour
1 teaspoon vanilla	1 teaspoon soda
1 egg	¼ teaspoon salt
2 1-ounce squares	1¼ cups milk
unsweetened chocolate,	Sweetened whipped cream
melted	or vanilla ice cream

Cream the butter and sugar. Add the vanilla and unbeaten egg; beat well. Stir in the cooled melted chocolate.

Sift the flour, soda, and salt. Add to the creamed mixture alternately with the milk, beating just until smooth.

Pour into a well-buttered and floured 1½-quart mold. Cover tightly and place on a rack over boiling water in a steamer or kettle. Cover and steam for 1 hour, or until it tests done with a pick inserted in the center. (Replenish the boiling water as needed.)

Let stand on a rack for 10 minutes, then unmold and serve warm with sweetened whipped cream or vanilla ice cream. Serves 8 to 10.

PUFF PUDDING

Puffy steamed individual currant puddings.

1 cup sifted all-purpose flour	½ cup milk
1 teaspoon baking powder	½ cup currants
1 tablespoon softened butter	Vanilla Sauce (recipe
1 egg	follows)

Sift the flour with the baking powder into a bowl. Cut in the butter to fine crumbs. Beat the egg well and stir in. Add the milk and currants. Beat well.

Turn into 4 well-buttered coffee cups, filling no more than one-half full. Place on a rack over boiling water in a steamer or a kettle. Cover and steam for 1 hour.

Unmold and serve warm in dessert bowls with chilled Vanilla Sauce poured over the tops. Serves 4.

Vanilla Sauce

¾ cup sugar	½ tablespoon butter
1 tablespoon flour	½ teaspoon vanilla
1 egg yolk	1 egg white
¾ cup plus 2 tablespoons milk	

Combine the sugar, flour, egg yolk, and the 2 tablespoons of milk in a bowl.

Heat the remaining ¾ cup of milk in a saucepan until bubbles appear around the edge. Gradually stir into the egg yolk mixture, then return to the saucepan. Cook, stirring over medium heat until the mixture comes to a boil. Continue cooking over low heat 2 or 3 minutes longer to take away the flour taste. Remove from the heat and stir in the butter, then the vanilla. Cover and chill.

When ready to serve, beat the egg white until stiff but moist peaks form. Fold into the chilled sauce.

Note: No sugar is called for in the pudding recipe, since the sauce is exceptionally sweet. Prepare the sauce before steaming the puddings to allow time for chilling.

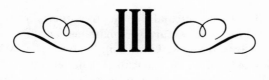

III

Cakes

DURING THE seventeenth and eighteenth centuries cakes were made from coarse flour. The texture was lightened either by beating to introduce air into the mix, by adding beaten eggs, or by adding yeast—and sometimes liquor—to cause the batter to rise. During this time American cooks made pound cakes, sponge cakes, and fruitcakes in the same way they were made in Europe.

The next hundred years gradually brought about a change. In the 1830s finely milled flour became widely available in America, and shortly after that wood-burning and coal-burning ovens became standard equipment. Within fifty years, gas ovens were common. That same era provided standardized measurers, improved beaters, and numerous American cookbooks. Most important of all was the discovery in the 1790s of pearl ash, which led to the marketing of baking powder in 1856. The availability of leavenings elevated the standard of cake baking from its European tradition and gave rise to the layer cake.

Enthusiastic American cooks experimented with flavors, fillings, and frostings to produce a significant change in the traditional concept of cake. Sponge cake and pound cake recipes were also revised and varied. Best of all, the angel food cake was created.

When, in the 1930s, hydrogenated shortening was introduced, the American cake revolution was fueled. Prior to that time, layer cakes were made with butter. The substitution of vegetable shortening permitted the use of additional sugar and additional liquid, which produced cakes that were both more tender and more finely grained.

Within ten years of its introduction, the new shortening also altered the standard for mixing cake batter. To the traditional method of creaming was added a "quick-mix" method that required only one bowl and reduced the process to two basic steps.

In 1948 a modified version of the "quick-mix" process led a commercial baker to create the chiffon cake, in which liquid shortening was used instead of solid shortening. About that same time packaged cake mixes were introduced to the American housewife.

What followed, unfortunately, was the virtual demise of the cake that was "made from scratch."

Cakes

Of all desserts, cakes require the most knowledge and exacting care to prepare successfully. Suggestions below will be helpful in preparing the cakes in this section.

1. Standard-size pans should be used: 8- or 9x1½-inch size for layers, and 9- or 10x4-inch size for loose-bottomed tube pans. Dimensions for a loaf pan are given in the recipes.

2. The preparation of the pans depends on the type of cake. For butter-type cakes, the bottom and sides of the pans should be well-greased with butter or vegetable shortening, then floured (shake out the excess). This preparation is necessary for the easy removal of the baked cake. Butter gives additional flavor, but salted butter may cause sticking. A better method, which ensures a smooth brown crust, is to cream together ½ cup of vegetable shortening with ¼ cup of flour, then rub this blend generously over the pan. The mixture can be stored at room temperature and used for subsequent cakes.

3. For delicate layer cakes, the pans are greased, then lined with waxed paper (cut to fit), which in turn is also greased. This procedure is also used for sponge cakes and mock-sponges if they are baked in layer pans, but the sides of the pans should not be greased.

4. Tube pans for sponge, angel food, and chiffon cakes are left ungreased so that the batter clings to the sides and rises to a high and airy state. The pan should be free of any trace of grease.

5. Butter (if used in the cake) should be at room temperature, but not so soft that it is oily. At this temperature it will be easier to cream initially and will blend better with the sugar. For fine texture the shortening and sugar should be beaten until fluffy or creamy, with the sugar granules almost dissolved. Although ordinary granulated sugar may be used, for the finest crumb and tenderness superfine sugar is preferred for delicate cakes.

6. Eggs should be at room temperature. If refrigerated, they will not beat to as high a volume. Whole eggs or egg yolks are often beaten until "thick and light or lemon-colored." This means until they are thickened sufficiently so that when the beaters are raised, they will fall back on themselves in a ribbon that slowly dissolves. If egg whites are to be beaten until stiff, they should be beaten only until they hold

stiff, moist points. Overbeaten and dry egg whites will be difficult to fold into the batter and will deflate considerably by the time they are sufficiently incorporated.

7. Flour should be sifted once before measuring, then sifted again with the remaining dry ingredients, not only to blend the ingredients but to incorporate air. For heavy-textured cakes one extra sifting may be enough, but for delicate cakes additional siftings are required. When directions require that the flour mixture be added alternately with the liquid, the dry ingredients should be added in thirds, the liquid in two parts, beginning and ending with the dry ingredients. This will prevent the batter from curdling. After each addition, the batter should be beaten only long enough to incorporate, and after the final addition only until well blended and smooth. Overbeating will deflate the air that has been incorporated into the egg mixture.

8. To prevent breaking, layer cakes are cooled for 5 to 10 minutes on racks before they are turned out of the pans. They are returned to the racks top side up to cool completely. The use of a rack prevents sogging; if inverted for cooling, the tops may stick to the racks.

9. Sponge, chiffon, and angel food cakes baked in tube pans are inverted and hung over a funnel (if the batter rises over the top of the pan) and allowed to cool completely before removing. This prevents excess shrinking during cooling and tearing the cake, which adheres firmly to the sides of the pan.

10. Pound cakes (like other butter-type cakes) and fruitcakes are removed from the pan when they have cooled sufficiently to be turned out without breaking. Pound cakes are then covered loosely with a cloth during the final cooling to prevent excess drying.

Frosting a Cake

1. Cakes that are to be frosted should be cooled to room temperature; the frosting will soften and run off if the cake is warm. (Loaf cakes that are cooled in the pan are an exception; recipes sometimes suggest frosting the cake immediately after baking.)

2. If necessary, lightly brush off any crumbs from the bottom and sides of the cake. If the crumbs are excessive, spread a thin layer of frosting, which has not completely thickened, over the cake to set the crumbs. This prevents them from mixing with the frosting.

3. If the cake is to be frosted on the serving plate (the easiest way), place four 3-inch strips of waxed paper crossed on the plate, leaving the center uncovered. The strips of paper will catch any drips and can be pulled out easily when the cake has been frosted and before it has set.

4. For layer cakes, place the first layer with the bottom side up on the plate. Frost, and then top with the second layer top side up. Frost the sides first in upward strokes, then the top. (If the layers are uneven in thickness, the thickest layer should be used for the bottom layer to make the difference in size less apparent.)

5. For loaf and tube pan cakes, invert on the serving plate. Frost the sides first, then the top.

SPONGE CAKE

Before the invention of leavening agents, cakes were raised by adding either yeast or many eggs that were whipped full of air. Those made with whipped eggs are called sponge cakes in America. Their history dates back several centuries in Europe, where they are known by other names, such as *genoise* in France, *genovese* in Italy, and *Biscuittorte* in Germany. This light cake is often used as a base for more elaborate desserts made with fruit and custard.

1 cup sifted cake flour	1 teaspoon vanilla
¼ teaspoon salt	5 egg whites
5 egg yolks	1 cup superfine sugar
2 tablespoons water	

Sift the flour and salt together 3 times.

Beat the egg yolks with an electric mixer on high speed until the mixture forms a ribbon when the beaters are withdrawn. Beat in the water and vanilla.

Beat the egg whites at high speed until soft peaks form. Gradually add the sugar and beat until stiff and glossy.

Fold the egg whites into the egg yolk mixture by hand alternately with the flour, a little at a time.

Turn the batter into an ungreased 9-inch tube pan. Bake in a 325° oven for 50 minutes, or until a pick comes out clean.

Invert the pan on a rack and allow it to cool for 1 hour. Loosen the cake with a spatula, then carefully remove from the pan. Let stand until completely cold.

Note: This is a small sponge cake suitable for separating into two layers to be used as a base for more elaborate desserts.

EGG YOLK SPONGE CAKE

The color of gold, this cake is a wonderful way to use leftover egg yolks. Angel Food Cake and Egg Yolk Sponge Cake were often made the same day.

1¼ cups sifted cake flour
1½ teaspoons baking powder
 1 teaspoon salt
12 egg yolks (¾ cup)

½ cup hot water
1 cup plus 2 tablespoons
 sugar
1½ teaspoons lemon extract

Sift the flour with the baking powder and salt 3 times.

Beat the egg yolks with an electric mixer at high speed until thick and lemon-colored. Gradually beat in the hot water.

Turn the speed to low and gradually beat in the sugar, then the lemon flavoring. Continue beating until the batter is thick again, then gradually beat in the flour mixture, beating only long enough to blend.

Turn into an ungreased 10-inch tube pan. Bake in a 325° oven for 60 to 65 minutes, or until the top springs back to the touch.

Invert and let hang on a funnel until cold (about 1½ hours).

To remove the cake from the pan, plunge a thin metal spatula down close against the edge of the pan; pull out and continue around the sides until the cake is loosened. Repeat around the center of the tube. (This cake is delicate and extra care must be used in the removal, or it will tear.)

To serve, cut into thick wedges with a very sharp knife, using a sawing motion. Serve plain or as an accompaniment to sweetened berries.

SPUNGE CAKE

Take the yolk of ten eggs, one pound of sugar; roll them well together; add the whites, after having beat them to a froth, with ten ounces of flour. It ought not to be put in until just before it is set in the oven.

—A New Family Receipt Book, Containing the Most Valuable Receipts
for the Various Branches of Cookery . . .
(1831)

HOT MILK CAKE

This cake has the light texture of sponge cake. It is a basic recipe that may be used for upside-down cake, served warm with whipped cream or sweetened crushed fruit. In this recipe it is split and filled with ice cream.

2 eggs	1 teaspoon baking powder
1 cup sugar	¼ teaspoon salt
½ cup milk	½ teaspoon vanilla
1 tablespoon butter	1 pint ice cream (any flavor)
1 cup sifted all-purpose flour	Confectioners' sugar

Beat the eggs with an electric mixer set at high speed until they are thick and lemon-colored and fall back, making a ribbon when the beaters are raised. Slowly add the sugar and beat at medium speed until thick and creamy.

Meanwhile, heat the milk slowly with the butter only until the butter is melted.

Sift the flour, baking powder, and salt together 3 times. Sift over the beaten egg mixture and quickly fold in by hand. Add the hot milk to the batter with the vanilla, folding in quickly just until blended.

Pour immediately into an 8-inch-square baking pan that has been greased and lined on the bottom only with greased waxed paper.

Bake at 350° for 25 to 30 minutes, or until the cake is golden and springs back to the touch.

Cool on a rack for 10 minutes, then loosen from the sides of the pan and turn out onto the rack. Cool completely.

To serve, split the cake into two layers with a serrated knife.

Beat the ice cream until soft enough to spread. Spread over the bottom layer and cover with the top layer. Dust the top with confectioners' sugar put through a sieve. Cut into squares and serve immediately. Serves 6.

JELLY ROLL

A traditional dessert cake that may be prepared with a variety of fillings, the simplest of which, jelly, is used here. This is not a true sponge cake, since it contains baking powder and butter. The eggs are beaten with the sugar over hot water.

¾ cup sifted cake flour	2 tablespoons melted butter
¾ teaspoon baking powder	1 teaspoon vanilla
¼ teaspoon salt	1 cup jelly (any flavor)
4 eggs	Confectioners' sugar
¾ cup superfine sugar	

Sift the flour, baking powder, and salt together.

Rinse a mixing bowl with hot water to warm it. Drain and dry it and set it over a smaller bowl containing hot water.

Break the eggs into the bowl and beat with an electric mixer set at medium speed, gradually adding the sugar in a steady stream. Continue beating until the mixture feels warm to the touch.

Remove the bowl from the smaller bowl and continue beating at high speed until the mixture forms a ribbon when the beaters are lifted.

Sift the flour mixture over the top, a third at a time, folding by hand only long enough to blend. Quickly fold in the melted butter and vanilla.

Turn into a greased 15x10x1-inch jelly roll pan that has been lined on the bottom with greased waxed paper. Spread the batter evenly. Bake in a 400° oven for 10 to 13 minutes, or until the cake springs back when lightly touched. (Do not overbake.)

Immediately invert the pan onto a cloth towel sprinkled with confectioners' sugar. Pull off the paper and spread the cake at once with the jelly or jam, which has been beaten with a fork if too stiff to spread. If the edges of the cake are crisp, trim with a sharp knife. Roll up from the long side.

Wrap in the towel and set, seam-side down, on a rack until cool (about 30 minutes). If desired, sprinkle with confectioners' sugar.

ANGEL FOOD CAKE

Angel food cake shares the top rank of popularity with sponge cakes and pound cakes. Of the three, only the angel food is of American origin. Invented in St. Louis, Missouri, in the 1880s, it has persisted as a favorite. It was originally called Angel's Food.

1 cup sifted cake flour	½ teaspoon salt
1½ cups sifted confectioners' sugar	1⅓ teaspoons cream of tartar
1⅓ cups egg whites (10 to 11)	⅔ cup superfine sugar
1½ teaspoons vanilla	Sweetened fruit or whipped
¼ teaspoon almond extract	cream (optional)

Sift the flour and confectioners' sugar together 3 times.

Beat the egg whites, vanilla, and almond extract with an electric mixer set at high speed until frothy. Add the salt and cream of tartar and continue beating until the peaks are almost stiff. Gradually beat in the superfine sugar, a little at a time, beating only long enough after each addition to incorporate the sugar.

After all the sugar is in, carefully fold in the flour mixture with a rubber spatula. Sift 4 tablespoons at a time over the egg white, folding after each addition only until the flour disappears. Do not overmix.

Carefully push the batter into an ungreased 9- or 10-inch tube pan. Run a knife through the batter in widening circles to break up any large air bubbles.

Bake in a 375° oven for 30 to 35 minutes, or until the cake looks dry on the top and springs back when lightly touched.

Invert the pan on a funnel and allow it to hang until cold (about 2 hours).

To remove the cake from the pan, run a sharp, thin-bladed knife around the pan in one long, steady stroke. Remove the bottom of the pan and release the tube in the same manner. Invert the cake onto a serving plate.

Cut slices with a sharp knife, using a sawing motion. Serve plain or topped with sweetened fruit or whipped cream.

ANGEL'S FOOD CAKE

One tumblerful of flour,
One tumblerful and a half of granulated sugar,
One teaspoonful of cream of tartar,
One teaspoonful of vanilla,
The Whites of eleven eggs.

Sift the flour four times; add the cream of tartar, and sift again. Sift the sugar four times. Beat the eggs to a stiff froth; then on the same platter, add the sugar lightly to them; then the flour slowly, and vanilla. Do not stop beating until the cake is put in the pan to bake. Bake forty minutes in a moderate oven. Turn the pan upside down to cool, and don't grease it before putting in the cake. The tumbler for measuring should hold about four gills and a quarter.

—The Kentucky Housewife, a Collection of Recipes for Cooking
by Mrs. Peter A. White (1885)

MARSHMALLOW CREAM CAKE

Like a white cake, yet reminiscent of angel food, this cake has a moist, velvety crumb and a delicate flavor. The unfrosted cake is known as Marshmallow Cream Cake, despite the lack of marshmallows in the recipe. To help justify the name, the frosting prescribed below includes the soft, white rascals.

2 cups sifted cake flour	½ teaspoon salt
2 cups sugar	1 teaspoon vanilla
¼ cup light cream	½ teaspoon almond extract
¾ cup milk	Marshmallow Frosting
6 egg whites	(recipe follows)
2 teaspoons baking powder	

Sift the flour and sugar together into a large mixing bowl.

Heat the cream and milk in a saucepan until bubbles appear around the edge. Gradually beat into the sugar and flour mixture with an electric mixer set at low speed. Continue beating until lukewarm.

Beat the egg whites until soft peaks form. Then add the baking powder and salt and continue beating until stiff but not dry.

Stir the vanilla and almond extract into the batter, then fold into the egg whites a little at a time with a rubber spatula. Fold after each addition only until blended.

Turn the batter into an ungreased 9- or 10-inch tube pan. Bake at 350° for 40 to 50 minutes, or until the cake is golden brown and the top springs back when lightly touched.

Invert the pan on a funnel and cool for 1 hour. Loosen the sides with a spatula and remove to a serving plate.

Frost the top and sides with Marshmallow Frosting.

Marshmallow Frosting

¾ cup white corn syrup	1 teaspoon vanilla
2 egg whites (¼ cup)	1 cup marshmallows (cut
⅛ teaspoon salt	fine)

Heat the corn syrup in a small saucepan until bubbles appear around the edge.

Beat the egg whites with an electric mixer until foamy. Add the salt and beat until stiff but not dry.

Slowly pour the hot syrup over the beaten egg whites. Continue beating until the mixture is fluffy and hangs in peaks from the beaters. Fold in the vanilla and marshmallows.

WHIPPED CREAM CAKE

Heavy cream replaces the butter in this delicate cream-colored layer cake frosted with a color-matched Butter Cream Frosting.

2 cups sifted cake flour	1 cup heavy cream
1½ cups sugar	½ cup cold water
3 teaspoons baking powder	½ teaspoon almond extract
½ teaspoon salt	Butter Cream Frosting
3 egg whites	(recipe follows)

Sift the flour with the sugar, baking powder, and salt 3 times.

Beat the egg whites until stiff but not dry.

Beat the cream until stiff, then carefully fold into the egg whites. Gradually fold in the water blended with the almond extract.

Fold the flour mixture into the egg white mixture one-third at a time, folding after each addition only until blended.

Turn into two greased 9-inch layer cake pans that have been lined on the bottom with greased waxed paper cut to fit.

Bake in a 350° oven for 25 to 30 minutes.

Cool on racks for 5 minutes, then turn out and carefully peel off the paper. Cool completely.

Frost and fill the layers with Butter Cream Frosting.

Butter Cream Frosting

¼ cup softened butter	3½ cups sifted confectioners'
2 egg yolks	sugar
¼ teaspoon salt	¼ cup milk (about)
1 teaspoon vanilla	

Cream the butter with the egg yolks, salt, and vanilla. Stir in 1 cup of the sugar and 3 tablespoons of the milk. Add the remaining sugar and beat until smooth. Add the remaining milk a teaspoonful at a time as needed, beating until the frosting holds its shape and is stiff enough to spread.

ALMOND CHIFFON CAKE

Chiffon cakes were developed and introduced by a leading flour manufacturer in 1948. They were promoted as the "first new cake in a hundred years." The distinguishing characteristic of this cake is that vegetable oil is used in place of solid shortening. It produces a high, airy cake that is appropriately named.

2¼ cups sifted cake flour	¾ teaspoon almond extract
1½ cups sugar	1 cup egg whites (7 to 8)
3 teaspoons baking powder	½ teaspoon cream of tartar
1 teaspoon salt	Butter Cream Frosting
½ cup vegetable oil	(recipe follows)
5 egg yolks	½ cup toasted, slivered
¼ cup cold water	blanched almonds
½ cup milk	

Sift the flour, sugar, baking powder, and salt into a mixing bowl. Make a well in the center and add the oil, egg yolks, water, milk, and almond extract. Beat until smooth.

Beat the egg whites with the cream of tartar until they form very stiff, but not dry, peaks.

Gradually add the egg yolk mixture to the whites, carefully folding in with a rubber spatula just until well blended.

Pour into an ungreased 10-inch tube pan. Bake at 325° for 55 minutes, then increase the heat to 350° and bake 10 to 15 minutes longer, or until the top springs back when lightly touched.

Invert the cake on a funnel and let hang until cold. To remove, carefully loosen with a spatula. Turn the pan over and hit the edge sharply on a table.

Frost the top and sides with Butter Cream Frosting, then garnish with the toasted almonds.

Butter Cream Frosting

1 cup sugar	2 egg whites
⅛ teaspoon cream of tartar	1 teaspoon vanilla
⅛ teaspoon salt	⅔ cup butter
¼ cup water	

Combine the sugar, cream of tartar, salt, and water in a saucepan. Bring to a boil and cook until a little of the mixture dropped into cold water forms a soft ball that holds its shape (240° on a candy thermometer).

Beat the egg whites until stiff but not dry. Add the syrup slowly to the egg whites, beating constantly. Add the vanilla. Cool thoroughly.

Cream the butter well. Add the egg white mixture to the butter 2 or 3 tablespoons at a time, beating well after each addition. Beat until of spreading consistency.

GOLD CUP CAKES

¼ cup vegetable shortening	¼ teaspoon salt
½ cup plus 2 tablespoons	¼ cup orange juice
sugar	2 tablespoons white vinegar
4 egg yolks	½ teaspoon orange extract
1 cup sifted cake flour	Orange Peel Frosting
½ teaspoon soda	(recipe follows)

Cream the shortening and sugar until light. Add the egg yolks one at a time, beating until fluffy.

Sift together the flour, soda, and salt. Add alternately with the orange juice mixed with the vinegar. Blend in the orange extract.

Spoon the batter into cupcake pans inserted with liners, filling them two-thirds full. Bake in a 375° oven for 18 to 20 minutes.

Cool a few minutes in the pans, then turn out. When completely cool, frost with Orange Peel Frosting. Makes 12 to 16 cupcakes.

Orange Peel Frosting

1 tablespoon soft butter	2 teaspoons lemon juice
2 teaspoons grated orange	1 teaspoon water
rind	
1 cup sifted confectioners'	
sugar	

Cream the butter with the orange rind. Gradually blend in one-third of the sugar. Add the remaining sugar alternately with the combined lemon juice and water, beating until smooth.

FEATHERY POUND CAKE

Neither a chiffon cake nor a pound cake, this cake has the lightness of the former and the flavor of the latter.

1 cup soft butter	3⅔ cups sifted cake flour
3 cups sugar	½ teaspoon salt
½ cup vegetable oil	1 cup milk
5 eggs	Vanilla Confectioners'
2 tablespoons lemon juice	Sugar (method follows)
2 teaspoons grated lemon	
rind	

Cream the butter well with an electric mixer set at medium speed. Slowly beat in the sugar and continue beating until light and fluffy (about 10 minutes). Gradually beat in the oil.

Add the eggs one at a time, beating 1½ minutes after each addition. Stir in the lemon juice and rind.

Sift the flour with the salt. Set aside ⅔ cup. Add the remaining flour alternately with the milk, beating after each addition only until blended.

Sprinkle the ⅔ cup of flour over the batter and fold in by hand gently, but thoroughly.

Turn the batter into a well-buttered 9- or 10-inch tube pan that has been lined on the bottom with greased waxed paper.

Bake in a 325° oven for 1 hour and 25 to 35 minutes, or until a pick inserted in the center comes out clean and the cake pulls away from the sides of the pan.

Transfer to a rack and cool for 20 minutes before loosening from the pan and turning out on the rack to cool. Cover loosely with a cloth towel while cooling to prevent drying. Then store in a covered container.

To serve, sprinkle the top with Vanilla Confectioners' Sugar (or plain confectioners' sugar) and slice thin. Makes about 24 slices.

Vanilla Confectioners' Sugar

1 dried vanilla bean	2 cups confectioners' sugar

Cut the vanilla bean in half, then split. Bury the pieces in the confectioners' sugar, cover tightly, and let stand for at least 24 hours—longer if desired.

Remove the vanilla bean (which may be used again). The remaining sugar may be kept and used whenever a dusting of the sugar is called for on any dessert.

POUND CAKE

The original English recipe for this rich cake called for a pound each of sugar, butter, eggs, and flour. Through the years the formula has been modified to improve the texture. This version has graham cracker crumbs for a topping. They are also used to dust the pan in which it is baked.

1 cup soft butter	½ teaspoon salt
1 cup sugar	¼ cup milk
4 eggs	1 teaspoon vanilla
2 cups sifted cake flour	¼ cup graham cracker
1 teaspoon baking powder	crumbs

Cream the butter well. Gradually add the sugar and beat at least 10 minutes with an electric mixer set at medium speed until the mixture looks like whipped cream.

Beat in the eggs one at a time, beating well after each addition (1½ minutes each at medium speed).

Sift the flour, baking powder, and salt together 3 times. With the electric mixer at low speed, add the dry ingredients alternately with the milk and vanilla, beginning and ending with the flour. Beat after each addition only until smooth.

Grease a 10x5x3-inch loaf pan generously with butter. Dust the pan with part of the graham cracker crumbs. Turn the batter into the prepared pan and sprinkle the remaining crumbs over the top; pat lightly.

Bake at 325° for 1 hour and 15 minutes, or until the cake tests done with a wooden pick inserted in the center. (The cake will split in the center, but this is characteristic.)

Let stand on a rack for 10 minutes, then remove and cool on the rack. When barely cool, wrap tightly and store at room temperature at least one day before serving for better flavor and texture. Cut into thin slices and serve plain.

Note: Properly protected in the wrapping and stored at room temperature, this cake will keep well for at least a week.

1-2-3-4 CAKE

Before the days of standardized measurements, cake ingredients were measured either by weight or by a tumbler or teacup. The same measure could be used for all ingredients, ensuring uniformity. The cake originally called for 1 measure of butter, 2 of sugar, 3 of flour, and 4 eggs. This basic cake formula was later revised to include milk and leavenings and became the forerunner of today's layer cakes.

1 cup soft butter	1 cup (less 2 tablespoons)
2 cups sugar	milk
4 eggs	2 tablespoons brandy
3 cups sifted cake flour	Lemon Brandy Frosting
3 teaspoons baking powder	(recipe follows)
½ teaspoon salt	

Cream the butter well with an electric mixer set at medium speed. Gradually add the sugar and continue beating at least 10 minutes until very light and fluffy.

Add the eggs one at a time, beating well after each addition (1½ minutes each at medium speed).

Sift the flour, baking powder, and salt together. Add alternately with the milk, beginning and ending with the flour. Beat only until smooth after each addition. Stir in the brandy.

Bake in three greased and floured 9-inch layer cake pans at 350° for 25 to 30 minutes, or until the cake springs back when lightly touched in the center.

Cool on racks for 5 minutes, then loosen at the edges and turn out onto the racks to finish cooling.

Fill and frost the layers with Lemon Brandy Frosting.

Lemon Brandy Frosting

2 lemons	½ cup softened butter
5 cups sifted confectioners'	1 teaspoon cream
sugar	2 tablespoons brandy

Coarsely grate the rind from the lemons. Wrap in a rinsed cheesecloth and squeeze the oil into 2 cups of the sugar. Let stand for 10 minutes. Reserve the lemons.

Beat the butter with the flavored sugar. Cut the lemons in half and squeeze the juice into the mixture through rinsed cheesecloth. Stir in the cream and brandy.

Beat in the remaining confectioners' sugar to a spreading consistency.

NUMBER CAKE

One tea cup full of butter, two tea cups full of sugar, three tea cups full of flour, four eggs, nutmeg, brandy.
—A New Family Receipt Book, Containing the Most Valuable Receipts
for the Various Branches of Cookery . . .
(1831)

GRAHAM CRACKER CAKE

Graham cracker crumbs replace the flour in this cake batter.

½ cup vegetable shortening
1 cup sugar
3 egg yolks
2 cups graham cracker
   crumbs
2 teaspoons baking powder
½ teaspoon salt
1 cup milk

3 egg whites
1 cup finely chopped walnuts

FILLING AND FROSTING
1 cup heavy cream
¼ cup confectioners' sugar
½ teaspoon vanilla
2 firm, ripe bananas

Cream the shortening and sugar until light and fluffy. Add the egg yolks one at a time, beating well after each addition.

Combine the graham cracker crumbs with the baking powder and salt. Add alternately to the creamed mixture with the milk, beginning and ending with the crumb mixture. Beat just until well blended after each addition.

Beat the egg whites until stiff. Fold in, then fold in the nuts.

Bake in two greased and floured 8-inch layer cake pans at 375° for 25 to 30 minutes or until the cake pulls away from the sides of the pan. Remove to cake racks and cool for 15 minutes before turning out. Cool completely.

When ready to serve, or an hour before, whip the cream with the confectioners' sugar and vanilla until stiff. Slice the bananas onto one layer and top with half the whipped cream. Add the second layer and spread the remaining whipped cream on top. (The sides are left unfrosted.)

NUTMEG CAKE

Nutmeg in the cake, and freshly grated nutmeg over a creamy lemon-flavored icing.

½ cup soft shortening (½ butter for flavor)	¼ teaspoon salt
1½ cups sugar	2 teaspoons freshly grated nutmeg
3 eggs	1 cup buttermilk
2 cups sifted all-purpose flour	½ teaspoon vanilla
1 teaspoon baking powder	Lemon Butter Frosting (recipe follows)
1 teaspoon soda	Freshly grated nutmeg

Cream the shortening. Gradually beat in the sugar and continue beating until well blended. Add the eggs one at a time, beating well after each addition.

Sift together the flour, baking powder, soda, salt, and nutmeg. Add the dry ingredients alternately with the combined buttermilk and vanilla, beating after each addition only until blended.

Pour into two well-greased and floured 9-inch round layer cake pans. Spread the batter evenly.

Bake in a 350° oven for about 25 minutes, or until a wooden pick comes out clean.

Cool on racks for 5 minutes, then turn out and cool completely. Frost the tops and sides with Lemon Butter Frosting. When assembled, grate nutmeg lightly over the top layer.

Lemon Butter Frosting

¼ cup soft butter	2 tablespoons water
2 egg yolks	2 tablespoons lemon juice
¼ teaspoon salt	
3½ cups sifted confectioners' sugar	

Cream the butter. Blend in the egg yolks, salt, and ½ cup of the sugar. Blend in the water and lemon juice. Add the remaining sugar and beat until smooth and stiff enough to hold its shape. (If necessary, beat in a little additional confectioners' sugar.)

MAN'S CAKE

What makes this Man's Cake? The flavor of strong coffee, perhaps. The texture is velvety despite the chopped pecans.

½ cup butter	1 cup cold strong coffee
1 cup sugar	¾ cup finely chopped pecans
2 eggs	1 teaspoon vanilla
2¼ cups sifted cake flour	Mocha Icing (recipe
2 teaspoons baking powder	follows)
½ teaspoon salt	

Cream the butter well. Gradually add the sugar and beat until light and fluffy. Beat in the eggs one at a time, beating well after each addition.

Sift the flour, baking powder, and salt together 3 times. Add alternately in thirds with the coffee, beginning and ending with the flour. Blend well, but do not overbeat.

Fold in the pecans and vanilla.

Turn the batter into two greased and floured 8-inch layer cake pans. Spread evenly, then spread the batter slightly up the sides so that the center is slightly lower.

Bake at 350° for 25 to 30 minutes, or until the cake shrinks from the sides of the pans.

Cool on racks for 5 minutes, then turn out and cool completely. Fill and frost with Mocha Icing.

Note: This cake will keep moist and fresh for several days in a covered cake container.

Mocha Icing

3 tablespoons soft butter	3 cups sifted confectioners'
1 teaspoon vanilla	sugar
⅛ teaspoon salt	3 tablespoons hot strong
5 tablespoons cocoa	coffee (about)

Blend the butter, vanilla, salt, and cocoa. Beat in ½ cup of the sugar. Add the hot coffee alternately with the remaining sugar, beating well after each addition. Add only enough coffee to make the icing of the right consistency to spread.

BOSTON CREAM PIE

An aura of confusion surrounds the naming of this two-layer cream-filled cake. Since the 1880s it has been called a pie. The term was perhaps applied when Boston was added to the title, since a half century before, cream puffs were called Boston Cream Cakes. The first Boston Cream Pies had a sprinkling of powdered sugar on top; the one most familiar today calls for chocolate icing. Boston's Parker House created this variation, listing it on their menus as Chocolate Cream Pie.

⅓ cup vegetable shortening
1 cup sugar
1 egg
1½ cups sifted all-purpose
  flour
2½ teaspoons baking powder
¼ teaspoon salt

⅔ cup milk
½ teaspoon vanilla
Cream Filling (recipe
follows)
Chocolate Icing (recipe
follows)

Cream the shortening and sugar until light and fluffy. Add the egg and beat until creamy.

Sift the flour, baking powder, and salt together. Add alternately with the combined milk and vanilla.

Turn the batter into a greased and floured 9-inch round layer cake pan. Bake in a 350° oven for about 30 minutes, or until the cake springs back when lightly touched in the center.

Cool on a rack for 5 minutes, then turn out and cool completely. Place the cake on a serving plate and split horizontally into two layers with a serrated knife. Carefully remove the top layer.

Fill with the chilled Cream Filling. Replace the top half and pour the warm Chocolate Icing over the top, spreading only to the edges. Chill. (When allowed to stand for several hours, the filling seeps into the cake, making the cake and filling seem almost as one.)

Cream Filling

½ cup sugar
3 tablespoons flour
¼ teaspoon salt
1½ cups milk

3 egg yolks
1 tablespoon butter
½ teaspoon vanilla

Combine the sugar, flour, and salt in a saucepan. Gradually stir in the milk. Cook over low heat, stirring until the mixture comes to a boil. Boil, stirring for 1 minute.

Beat the egg yolks slightly. Gradually stir in about half the thickened sauce. Return to the heat and cook, stirring 2 or 3 minutes longer to take away the flour taste.

Remove from the heat and blend in the butter. Strain into a bowl. Cool for a few minutes, then blend in the vanilla. Cover and cool, then chill.

Chocolate Icing

2 1-ounce squares
  unsweetened chocolate
2 tablespoons vegetable
  shortening

1 cup sifted confectioners'
  sugar
2 tablespoons hot water
½ teaspoon vanilla

Melt the chocolate and shortening in a small skillet over very low heat. Remove from the heat and blend in the sugar and hot water. Stir until smooth and slightly thickened (do not beat). Stir in the vanilla. Use immediately.

A lady says that to prevent cake from falling, lift it up, and let it drop suddenly to the table after putting it in the tin. The air-bubbles will rise and when baking there will be no falling.

—Mrs. Owens' Cook Book and Useful Household Hints
by Frances E. Owens, 1888 Revised Edition (1884)

FRESH COCONUT CAKE

A fresh coconut is required to make this delicious cake. The grated coconut meat enriches the batter and is used to garnish the fluffy egg white frosting. Directions for preparing a fresh coconut are given at the end of the recipe.

½ cup butter	¼ teaspoon salt
1½ cups sugar	Fresh coconut milk and
3 eggs	sweet milk to make 1 cup
2½–3 cups fresh grated coconut	½ teaspoon vanilla
(loosely packed)	½ teaspoon almond extract
2½ cups sifted cake flour	Fluffy White Frosting
3 teaspoons baking powder	(recipe follows)

Cream the butter well. Add the sugar gradually and beat until light and fluffy. Add the eggs one at a time, beating well after each addition. Stir in 1 cup of the coconut.

Sift the flour, baking powder, and salt together 3 times. Add the flour mixture in thirds alternately with the combined coconut milk and sweet milk, beating just long enough after each addition to blend well. Blend in the vanilla and almond extract.

Pour into two well-greased and floured 9-inch round layer cake pans. Shake the pans slightly to level the batter.

Bake in a 375° oven for 25 to 30 minutes, or until the tops spring back when lightly touched.

Cool in the pans on racks for 5 minutes, then turn out. Return to the racks and cool completely.

Layer the cakes, filling and frosting with Fluffy White Frosting. Sprinkle the tops and sides with the remaining 1½ to 2 cups of grated coconut. (Do not garnish too heavily, or the coconut will pull the frosting from the sides of the cake.)

Fluffy White Frosting

2 egg whites	¼ teaspoon cream of tartar
¾ cup sugar	¼ teaspoon salt
⅓ cup light corn syrup	½ teaspoon vanilla
2 tablespoons water	¼ teaspoon almond extract

Combine the egg whites, sugar, corn syrup, water, cream of tartar, and salt in the top of a double boiler.

Cook over rapidly boiling water, beating with a rotary beater or electric mixer until the mixture stands in soft peaks.

Remove from the heat and add the vanilla and almond extract. Continue beating until very stiff and cool. Work quickly when placing on the cake as this frosting tends to dry.

Note: This cooked frosting, though more involved in the making than similar uncooked egg white frostings, has good keeping qualities. It will hold for a day or two without separating, the syrup seeping into the cake.

To prepare fresh coconut: Puncture two of the eyes (soft spots) at the end of the coconut with an ice pick or screwdriver. Drain the liquid and strain to remove any traces of the brown skin.

Place the drained coconut in a 400° oven for 15 minutes, or until it splits open. Remove and allow it to cool.

Break the coconut into several pieces with a mallet or a hammer. Pry the white meat loose from the shell if necessary. Trim off the brown husk with a vegetable peeler.

Grate the meat by hand, in a blender, or in a food processor.

Note: A medium-size coconut will provide about 4 cups of loosely packed coconut.

A delightful flavoring for cake is obtained by placing a geranium leaf in the bottom of a cake-tin and pouring the cake over it.

—Mrs. Owens' Cook Book and Useful Household Hints
by Frances E. Owens, 1888 Revised Edition (1884)

BUTTERSCOTCH CAKE

This cake belongs to a family of cakes variously referred to as "one-bowl," "quick-mix," or "magic" cakes. They differ from conventional cakes by the method in which they are mixed and by the use of vegetable shortening instead of butter. Cakes of this type were the predecessors of packaged cake mixes. For other cakes in this family, refer to Quick-Mix Cakes in the Index.

2 cups sifted cake flour	1 cup milk
3 teaspoons baking powder	1 teaspoon vanilla
1 teaspoon salt	2 eggs
1½ cups light brown sugar (packed)	Browned Butter Frosting (recipe follows)
½ cup vegetable shortening	

Sift the flour, baking powder, and salt together into a mixing bowl.

Add the brown sugar, shortening, ⅔ cup of the milk, and the vanilla. Beat 2 minutes with an electric mixer set at medium speed.

Add the remaining ⅓ cup of milk and the unbeaten eggs. Beat 2 minutes longer.

Pour into two greased and floured 8-inch round layer cake pans. Bake at 350° for about 30 minutes, or until the cake tests done with a wooden pick and springs back to the touch.

Cool for 5 minutes on racks, then turn out and cool completely. Fill and frost with Browned Butter Frosting.

Browned Butter Frosting

6 tablespoons butter	⅛ teaspoon salt
3 cups sifted confectioners' sugar	3½ tablespoons cream (about)

Heat the butter in a saucepan with 1 cup of the sugar and the salt until it turns a nut-brown color. Remove from the heat.

Add the remaining sugar and the cream alternately, beating until very smooth and of spreading consistency.

*Who can resist
one of America's favorite desserts—
a light and airy Angel Food Cake (page 80),
here served with luscious plump strawberries?*

BLITZ TORTE

Sometimes called Lightning Cake, this old-time cake has a layer each of cake batter and meringue baked together.

CAKE
½ cup butter
½ cup sugar
4 egg yolks
1⅓ cups sifted cake flour
1½ teaspoons baking powder
¼ teaspoon salt
5 tablespoons milk
1 teaspoon vanilla

MERINGUE AND TOPPING
4 egg whites
1 cup plus 1 tablespoon sugar
½ teaspoon cinnamon
½ cup slivered almonds

FILLING
1 cup heavy cream

To make the cake, cream the butter well. Gradually add the sugar and beat until light and fluffy. Add the egg yolks one at a time, beating well after each addition.

Sift the flour with the baking powder and salt 3 times. Add the dry ingredients alternately with the combined milk and vanilla, beating well. (The batter will be stiff.)

Spread the batter in the bottoms of two greased and floured 8-inch round layer cake pans.

To make the meringue, beat the egg whites until soft peaks form, then gradually add the cup of sugar and beat until stiff and glossy. Spread and smooth evenly over the cake batter.

Combine the remaining tablespoon of sugar with the cinnamon and sprinkle over the tops. Then scatter the almonds over, pressing in lightly.

Bake in a 350° oven for 30 to 35 minutes, or until the cake tests done and the meringue is set.

Remove from the oven and cool completely on racks before removing from the pans. When cooled, loosen and remove the layers. (To prevent the almonds from falling off, cover with a piece of waxed paper before inverting.)

Place one layer, meringue side up, on a serving plate. Whip the cream and spread it over the top. Add the second layer, also meringue side up. Chill for at least 1 hour before serving.

COLD WATER CAKE

This white cake takes a lot of sifting and careful beating to make it light as a feather. The result is well worth the effort.

1 cup superfine sugar
1 cup sifted confectioners' sugar
2½ cups sifted cake flour
2 teaspoons baking powder
¼ teaspoon salt
½ cup butter

1 teaspoon vanilla
1 cup cold water
4 egg whites
¼ teaspoon cream of tartar
Creamy White Frosting (recipe follows)

Sift the sugars together 4 times. Sift the flour, baking powder, and salt together 3 times.

Cream the butter well with an electric mixer set at medium speed. Gradually beat in the combined sugars, then add the vanilla and 2 tablespoons of the water. Continue beating until very light and creamy.

With the mixer on low, add the flour mixture alternately with the remaining water, beginning and ending with the flour. Beat only until blended after each addition; overbeating will reduce the volume of the cake.

Beat the egg whites until foamy, then add the cream of tartar and beat until they stand in stiff, moist peaks.

Stir about 1 cup of the egg whites into the batter to lighten it, then fold in the remainder with a rubber spatula.

Turn into two greased and floured 9-inch round layer cake pans. Bake at 350° for about 30 minutes, or until the tops spring back when lightly touched.

Cool on racks for 10 minutes, then turn out and return to the racks to cool completely.

Fill the layers and frost the top and sides with Creamy White Frosting.

Creamy White Frosting

½ cup milk
4 teaspoons cornstarch
¼ teaspoon salt
¼ cup butter

¼ cup vegetable shortening
1 teaspoon vanilla
3 cups sifted confectioners' sugar

Combine the milk, cornstarch, and salt in a small saucepan.

Cook, stirring until the mixture boils and is clear. Remove from the heat and cool.

In a mixing bowl, combine the shortenings and beat until creamy. Gradually add the cornstarch mixture and the vanilla. Add the sugar little by little and continue beating until the frosting is the consistency of stiffly whipped cream.

Note: This frosting is not overly sweet and stays creamy.

WASHINGTON PIE

The first jelly cakes were based on the 1-2-3-4 Cake. Several thin layers were stacked, jelly was spread between the layers, and the top was sprinkled with sugar. Later versions, like the Washington Pie described here, are made from a one- or two-egg cake recipe and have only two layers. For a special decorative effect, a lace paper doily was laid over the top and confectioners' sugar was pressed on with a spoon. Then the doily was removed.

2 cups sifted cake flour	¾ cup milk
2½ teaspoons baking powder	1 egg
½ teaspoon salt	
1 cup sugar	**FILLING AND TOPPING**
⅓ cup vegetable shortening	Red raspberry preserves
1 teaspoon vanilla	Confectioners' sugar

Sift the flour, baking powder, salt, and sugar into a mixing bowl. Add the shortening, vanilla, and ½ cup of the milk. Beat for 2 minutes with an electric mixer set at medium speed, or 300 strokes by hand.

Add the remaining milk and the egg. Beat 2 minutes longer, scraping the bowl often.

Pour the batter into two well-greased and floured 8-inch layer cake pans. Bake at 350° for 25 to 30 minutes, or until the top springs back when lightly touched.

Cool on a rack for 5 minutes, then turn out onto the rack and cool completely.

Spread one layer generously with the raspberry preserves, top with the second layer, and press the confectioners' sugar through a sieve to lightly cover the top. Serves 6 to 8.

HICKORY NUT CAKE

A popular white layer cake in areas where wild hickory nuts grow: the cake is also good when pecans are substituted.

½ cup butter	1 teaspoon vanilla
¼ cup vegetable shortening	1 cup finely chopped hickory
2 cups sugar	nuts or pecans
2½ cups sifted cake flour	5 egg whites
2½ teaspoons baking powder	Maple Frosting (recipe
1 teaspoon salt	follows)
1 cup milk	

Beat the shortenings and sugar together until creamy.

Sift the flour, baking powder, and salt together 3 times. Add to the butter mixture alternately with the combined milk and vanilla in thirds, beginning and ending with the dry ingredients. Blend the nuts with the last portion of flour before adding. Beat only until well blended.

Beat the egg whites until stiff but not dry. Stir about a cup of the egg whites into the batter to lighten it, then fold in the remainder.

Turn into two greased and floured 9-inch round layer cake pans. Spread the batter evenly. Bake at 350° for 30 minutes, or until the cake pulls away from the sides of the pan. Cool for 5 minutes on racks, then turn out and cool completely.

Layer the cakes, filling and frosting the tops and sides with Maple Frosting. Garnish the top with additional chopped nuts if desired.

Maple Frosting

6 tablespoons soft butter	6 tablespoons maple syrup
3 cups sifted confectioners'	
sugar	

Cream the butter and sugar together to make a smooth paste. Gradually stir in the maple syrup. Beat until of spreading consistency.

POPPY SEED CAKE

Incorporating poppy seeds into cake or pastry is an old European custom, now also American by adoption. Spread through this white cake batter, the seeds impart color as well as a delicate nut flavor.

½ cup (about 2½ ounces) poppy seeds
¾ cup milk
¾ cup (1½ sticks) butter
1½ cups sugar
1 teaspoon vanilla
2¼ cups sifted cake flour
2 teaspoons baking powder
½ teaspoon salt
4 egg whites
Cream Filling (recipe follows)
Fluffy White Frosting (page 94)

Soak the poppy seeds in the milk for at least 2 hours, or overnight if preferred.

Cream the butter with the sugar and vanilla until light and fluffy.

Sift together the flour, baking powder, and salt. Add a third at a time to the creamed mixture alternately with the milk and poppy seeds. Beat only until smooth after each addition.

Beat the egg whites until rounded peaks are formed and the whites do not slide from the bowl when inverted. Carefully spread them over the batter and gently fold in by hand.

Turn the batter into two greased and lightly floured 8-inch round layer cake pans. Bake at 350° for 30 to 35 minutes.

Cool on racks for 10 minutes, then turn out and cool completely. Fill with the chilled Cream Filling and frost the tops and sides with the Fluffy White Frosting.

Cream Filling

¼ cup sugar
1 tablespoon cornstarch
¼ teaspoon salt
1 cup milk
4 egg yolks
1 teaspoon vanilla

Combine the sugar, cornstarch, and salt in a saucepan. Gradually stir in the milk. Slowly bring to a boil over direct heat, stirring constantly. Boil for 1 minute.

Remove from the heat and stir about half the mixture into the egg yolks. Return to the saucepan and cook, stirring 1 minute longer.

Cool slightly, then stir in the vanilla. Cover and cool, then refrigerate until well chilled.

MARY TODD'S WHITE CAKE

The basic recipe on which all white butter cakes of today are based is reported to have been invented by Monsieur Giron, a Lexington, Kentucky, caterer, on the occasion of Lafayette's last visit to America in the 1820s. He decorated his cake with flags made of colored sugar. After that introduction, every famous cake baker in the bluegrass region began making white butter cakes, frosting and filling them at personal discretion. The recipe that has become most famous of all originated in the household of Mary Todd's ancestors. When Mary Todd served her version of this cake to Abraham Lincoln, he is said to have remarked that it was the best white cake in Kentucky. The cake contains chopped almonds and is frosted with a boiled frosting to which candied pineapple and cherries have been added.

1 cup soft butter	1 cup milk
2 cups sugar	1 cup finely chopped
½ teaspoon salt	blanched almonds
1 teaspoon vanilla	6 egg whites
3 cups sifted cake flour	Mary Todd's Frosting
3 teaspoons baking powder	(recipe follows)

Cream the butter until very soft. Gradually beat in the sugar, salt, and vanilla, and continue beating until light and fluffy.

Sift the flour with the baking powder 3 times. Add alternately in thirds to the creamed mixture with the milk, beginning and ending with the flour. Blend the nuts with the last portion of flour before adding. Beat only until well blended.

Beat the egg whites until stiff. Spread over the batter and carefully but quickly fold in just until blended.

Turn the batter into a well-greased and floured 9- or 10-inch tube pan. Bake at 350° for 50 to 60 minutes, or until the cake shrinks slightly from the pan.

Set on a rack to cool for 15 minutes, then loosen the cake if necessary and turn out. Invert onto the rack to cool completely. Frost the top and sides with Mary Todd's Frosting.

Mary Todd's Frosting

2 cups sugar	1 cup water

¼ teaspoon salt	½ cup finely cut candied
1 teaspoon vinegar	cherries
2 egg whites	½ cup finely cut candied
½ teaspoon almond extract	pineapple

Combine the sugar, water, salt, and vinegar in a saucepan. Cook over medium heat, stirring just until the sugar is dissolved.

Continue cooking without stirring until the syrup forms a 6- to 8-inch thread when dropped from the tip of a spoon (240° on a candy thermometer).

While the syrup cooks, beat the egg whites until stiff enough to hold peaks. Pour the hot syrup very slowly into the egg whites, beating constantly until the frosting holds its shape. Beat in the almond extract.

Fold in the candied cherries and pineapple.

There are really but two elementary forms of cake—that made with butter, known as pound cake, and that made without butter, known as sponge cake. The modification of pound cake, in which the proportion of flour is increased with the addition of milk, is called cup-cake, and this makes the basis of almost all the plain and layer cakes. . . .

—Washburn-Crosby Co's New Gold Medal Cookbook
(1904)

LANE CAKE

Lane Cake is a three-layer white cake, with a golden filling containing raisins, pecans, and coconut. The source of the name is obscure, but the cake is said to have originated in Alabama, where it remains a favorite at Christmas.

1 cup butter	¾ teaspoon salt
2 cups sugar	½ cup milk
1 teaspoon vanilla	½ cup water
3¼ cups sifted all-purpose flour	8 egg whites
3½ teaspoons baking powder	Lane Cake Filling (recipe follows)

Cream the butter until light. Gradually add the sugar, beating until light and creamy. Beat in the vanilla.

Sift the flour, baking powder, and salt together 3 times. Add to the creamed mixture alternately with the combined milk and water, beating after each addition just until blended.

Beat the egg whites until they stand in stiff, glossy peaks. Stir about one-fourth of the egg whites into the creamed mixture, then fold in the remainder gently just until blended.

Divide the batter evenly among three 9-inch round layer cake pans, which have been greased and lined on the bottoms with greased waxed paper.

Bake in a 350° oven for 20 to 25 minutes, or until the tops spring back when lightly touched.

Cool on cake racks for 5 minutes. Carefully loosen around the edges with a spatula, then turn out on racks. Peel off the waxed paper gently. Cool completely, then spread Lane Cake Filling between the layers and on top only.

Cover and store in a cool place for a day or two to mellow before serving.

Lane Cake Filling

8 egg yolks	2 tablespoons light corn syrup
1½ cups sugar	

½ cup soft butter	1 cup chopped seeded raisins
⅓ cup brandy	1 cup shredded coconut
1 teaspoon vanilla	2 cups chopped pecans

Beat the egg yolks with the sugar until the mixture is thick and lemon-colored and falls back into a ribbon when the beaters are raised.

Turn into the top of a double boiler and add the corn syrup and soft butter. Set over simmering water and cook, stirring constantly until the sugar is dissolved, the butter is melted, and the mixture thickens slightly. It should appear almost translucent.

Remove from the heat and blend in the brandy and vanilla. Stir in the raisins, coconut, and pecans. Cool before using.

Variation: For a more colorful frosting, substitute 1 cup of quartered candied cherries for 1 cup of the pecans.

MARKING CAKES IN GOLD
Bake round cakes for the children, and when the frosting is hard, dip a small brush into the yolk of an egg, and write a word or name upon the cake. It pleases the little ones very much.

—Miss Parloa's New Cook Book and Marketing Guide
by Miss Maria Parloa (1880)

LADY BALTIMORE CAKE

Lady Baltimore Cake is perhaps the best known of all cakes named for famous people. It is said to have been created by Mrs. Alicia Rhett Mayberry of Charleston, South Carolina, and was immortalized when Owen Wister described it and used its name for the title of his book, *Lady Baltimore*, published in 1906. It has remained popular, particularly through the South, for many decades. The cake has a white layer base that is frosted with a cooked white frosting. Fillings vary, but most combine some of the frosting with nuts, raisins, and figs, as does this version.

½ cup butter	½ cup water
1½ cups sugar	½ teaspoon vanilla
3 cups sifted cake flour	¼ teaspoon almond extract
3 teaspoons baking powder	6 egg whites (¾ cup)
¼ teaspoon salt	Lady Baltimore Frosting
½ cup milk	and Filling (recipe follows)

Cream the butter and sugar with an electric mixer set at medium speed until it looks like whipped cream.

Sift the flour, baking powder, and salt together 3 times. Add alternately at low speed to the creamed mixture with the combined milk, water, and flavorings. Beat only until blended after each addition.

Beat the egg whites until stiff but still moist. Spread them carefully over the batter. Fold in by hand just until blended.

Turn the batter into two greased 9-inch layer cake pans that have been lined on the bottom with greased waxed paper.

Bake at 350° for 25 to 30 minutes, or until the centers spring back when lightly touched.

Allow the cakes to remain in the pans for at least 5 minutes after they have been removed from the oven. Turn out and carefully remove the waxed paper, then cool completely.

Fill and frost with Lady Baltimore Frosting and Filling.

Lady Baltimore Frosting and Filling

2 egg whites (⅓ cup)   1½ cups sugar

⅓ cup water
1½ teaspoons light corn syrup
½ teaspoon salt
1 teaspoon vanilla

6 dried figs
½ cup raisins
⅓ cup pecans

Combine the egg whites, sugar, water, corn syrup, and salt in the top of a double boiler. Beat 1 minute with an electric mixer set at medium speed.

Set the pan over rapidly boiling water and continue beating until the mixture holds stiff peaks (about 5 to 7 minutes).

Remove from the boiling water, add the vanilla, and continue beating until the mixture is thick enough to spread.

Chop the figs, raisins, and pecans. Combine and add enough of the frosting so that it will spread easily. Fill the cake with this mixture, then frost the top and sides with the remainder of the frosting.

Cake also should be kept in a tight tin box. Tin boxes made with covers like trunks, with handles at the ends, are best for bread and cake.

—Miss Beecher's Housekeeper and Healthkeeper
by Catharine E. Beecher (1873)

LORD BALTIMORE CAKE

The history of this famous cake is not as clear as that of Lady Baltimore Cake. It is thought to have been named for George Calvert, Lord Baltimore, the English statesman who founded the colony of Maryland. It is an elaborate cake made with egg yolks and flavored with liquor. As with Lady Baltimore Cake, a fluffy frosting is used, but here it is sweetened with brown sugar. The filling contains macaroon crumbs, pecans, and candied cherries.

¾ cup (1½ sticks) butter
1¼ cups sugar
8 egg yolks
2½ cups sifted cake flour
4 teaspoons baking powder
½ teaspoon salt

¾ cup milk
½ teaspoon lemon extract
2 tablespoons whiskey or
rum
Lord Baltimore Frosting
and Filling (recipe follows)

Cream the butter well with an electric mixer set at medium speed. Gradually add the sugar and beat until light and fluffy. Add the egg yolks one at a time, beating well after each addition. Continue beating until thick and lemon-colored.

Sift the flour with the baking powder and salt 3 times.

With the mixer set at lowest speed, add the flour mixture alternately with the milk in thirds, beginning and ending with the flour. Blend in the lemon extract and the whiskey or rum. (Do not overmix.)

Turn into two greased and lightly floured 9-inch round layer cake pans. Bake at 350° for 25 to 30 minutes, or until the cake springs back when lightly touched in the center.

Cool for 10 minutes on racks, then turn out and return to the racks to finish cooling.

Put the layers together with Lord Baltimore Frosting and Filling.

Lord Baltimore Frosting and Filling

Lady Baltimore Frosting
and Filling (page 106)
1½ cups brown sugar (firmly
packed)

½ cup macaroon crumbs
½ cup chopped pecans
12 chopped candied cherries

Prepare the recipe for Lady Baltimore Frosting, but substitute the brown sugar for the sugar, and the macaroons, pecans, and cherries for the figs, raisins, and pecans in the filling.

Combine the macaroon crumbs, pecans, and cherries with enough of the frosting to make a good spreading consistency. Fill the cake with this mixture, then frost the top and sides with the remainder of the frosting.

CRUMB CAKE

This old-time Pennsylvania Dutch specialty is served either as a dessert or with coffee for breakfast.

2 cups light brown sugar (packed)	1 teaspoon soda
2 cups sifted all-purpose flour	1 cup sour milk or buttermilk
½ cup butter or margarine	¼ teaspoon salt
1 egg	1 teaspoon vanilla
	Cinnamon

Combine the brown sugar, flour, and butter or margarine, cutting in the shortening with a pastry blender or your fingers until the mixture is crumbly. Remove 1 cup and reserve for the topping.

Beat the egg lightly and add to the remaining crumbs. Dissolve the soda in the milk, then add along with the salt and vanilla. Beat the mixture only until smooth.

Pour into a greased and floured 9-inch-square baking pan. Sprinkle the remaining crumbs over the batter and sprinkle lightly with cinnamon.

Bake at 350° for 40 to 45 minutes, or until a wooden pick inserted in the center comes out clean.

Cool in the pan on a rack. Cut into squares to serve.

WHITE CHOCOLATE CAKE

An unusual cake. The color is white, but the flavor is reminiscent of chocolate. It is made with white chocolate, which is sold in irregular chunks at a confectionary.

¼ pound white chocolate	1 teaspoon soda
1 cup butter	1 cup buttermilk
2 cups sugar	1 cup finely chopped pecans
4 eggs	White Chocolate Butter
1 teaspoon vanilla	Frosting (recipe follows)
2½ cups sifted cake flour	

Chop the chocolate into small pieces and melt over hot water. Cool slightly.

Cream the butter well. Gradually add the sugar and beat until light and fluffy.

Add the eggs one at a time, beating well after each addition. Blend in the vanilla and the slightly cooled chocolate.

Sift the flour with the soda, then add alternately with the buttermilk to the creamed mixture, beating just until blended after each addition. Stir in the pecans.

Pour the batter into three greased and floured 9-inch layer cake pans, spreading evenly.

Bake at 350° for 25 to 30 minutes, or until the tops spring back when lightly touched.

Cool in the pans for 10 minutes on racks, then turn out to finish cooling. Fill and frost the layers with White Chocolate Butter Frosting.

White Chocolate Butter Frosting

½ cup soft butter	2 egg yolks
4 cups sifted confectioners' sugar	2 teaspoons vanilla
¼ pound white chocolate, melted	⅓ cup light cream

Cream the butter and 1 cup of the sugar. Add the slightly cooled melted chocolate, egg yolks, and vanilla and beat thoroughly. Stir in the remaining sugar and the cream. Beat until creamy and of spreading consistency, adding additional cream if needed.

SWISS CHOCOLATE CAKE

A pale chocolate loaf cake frosted with color-matched cream cheese frosting.

1 1-ounce square unsweetened chocolate	2 cups sifted cake flour
½ cup vegetable shortening	2½ teaspoons baking powder
1 teaspoon vanilla	¾ teaspoon salt
1¼ cups sugar	1 cup heavy cream
2 eggs	Swiss Chocolate Frosting (recipe follows)

Melt the chocolate over hot water. Cool slightly.

Cream the shortening with the vanilla. Gradually add the sugar and beat until light and fluffy.

Add the eggs, one at a time, beating well after each addition. Blend in the cooled chocolate.

Sift the flour, baking powder, and salt together. Add alternately with the cream in thirds, beating only until smooth after each addition.

Line the bottom of a greased 9-inch-square baking pan with waxed paper and grease the waxed paper. Turn the batter into the prepared pan. Bake at 350° for 30 to 35 minutes.

Cool for at least 10 minutes in the pan, then turn out and carefully peel off the waxed paper. Cool completely, then frost the top and sides with Swiss Chocolate Frosting.

Swiss Chocolate Frosting

1 3-ounce package cream cheese	1 1-ounce square unsweetened chocolate
1 tablespoon milk	¼ teaspoon salt
2 cups sifted confectioners' sugar	½ teaspoon vanilla

Soften the cream cheese to room temperature. Blend in the milk. Gradually beat in the confectioners' sugar.

Melt the chocolate over hot water. Add to the cheese mixture along with the salt and vanilla. Beat until creamy.

DUCK POINT CAKE

A chocolate loaf cake flavored with cinnamon, frosted while hot and served warm. The recipe comes from the coastal area of South Carolina.

½ cup (1 stick) margarine	1 teaspoon cinnamon
¼ cup cocoa	1 teaspoon soda
1 cup water	½ cup buttermilk
2 cups unsifted all-purpose flour	2 eggs
2 cups sugar	Cocoa Pecan Frosting (recipe follows)

Combine the margarine, cocoa, and water in a saucepan. Stir over low heat until the margarine is melted.

Sift the flour, sugar, and cinnamon together into the bowl of an electric mixer. Add the melted cocoa mixture. Beat at medium speed for 2 minutes.

Dissolve the soda in the buttermilk; add along with the unbeaten eggs. Continue beating 2 minutes longer, scraping the beaters and bowl often.

Pour the batter into a buttered 13x9-inch baking pan. Bake at 350° for 40 to 45 minutes.

While the cake is baking, prepare the Cocoa Pecan Frosting. When the cake comes out of the oven, let it stand for 10 minutes, then spread the top with the frosting. Cut into squares and serve while warm.

Cocoa Pecan Frosting

½ cup (1 stick) margarine	1 pound confectioners' sugar, sifted
¼ cup cocoa	1 cup chopped pecans
5½ tablespoons milk	

Melt the margarine in a saucepan. Remove from the heat and stir in the cocoa and milk. Gradually beat in the confectioners' sugar, beating until the mixture is smooth and well blended. Stir in the pecans. Let stand until ready to frost the cake.

GYPSY LISETTE

A cocoa spice cake.

½ cup vegetable shortening
¼ cup butter
1½ cups sugar
3 eggs
1¾ cups sifted all-purpose
    flour
2 tablespoons cocoa
½ teaspoon baking powder
½ teaspoon soda
½ teaspoon salt

1 teaspoon cinnamon
¾ teaspoon nutmeg
¾ cup buttermilk
1 teaspoon vanilla
½ teaspoon lemon extract
¼ cup chopped English
    walnuts
¼ cup chopped pecans
    Creole Frosting (recipe
    follows)

Cream the shortenings together. Gradually beat in the sugar and continue beating until fluffy.

Add the eggs one at a time, beating until light and creamy.

Sift the flour, cocoa, baking powder, soda, salt, cinnamon, and nutmeg together 3 times. Add alternately to the creamed mixture with the combined buttermilk, vanilla, and lemon extract, beginning and ending with the flour. Blend the nuts with the last portion of flour before adding. Beat just until well blended.

Turn into two greased and floured 9-inch round layer cake pans. Bake at 350° for 25 to 30 minutes. Cool for 10 minutes on cake racks, then turn out and cool completely.

Frost and fill the layers with the Creole Frosting.

Creole Frosting

8 tablespoons butter
1 egg yolk
4 cups sifted confectioners'
    sugar

5 teaspoons cocoa
1 teaspoon cinnamon
2 tablespoons cold coffee

Soften the butter to room temperature. Blend in the egg yolk, 1 cup of the sugar, the cocoa, the cinnamon, and the coffee. Add the remaining sugar and beat until smooth and stiff enough to hold its shape. (If necessary, beat in a little additional confectioners' sugar.)

WELLESLEY FUDGE CAKE

Fondly remembered by scores of Wellesley College students who left the campus as often as possible to feast on this delectable cake in the Wellesley Tea Room in town. The version that follows, however, is credited to the kitchens of the Waldorf-Astoria Hotel in Manhattan in the 1950s.

3 1-ounce squares	½ teaspoon salt
unsweetened chocolate	2 teaspoons vanilla
½ cup butter	1½ cups milk
2 cups sugar	1 cup finely chopped pecans
2 eggs	or English walnuts
2 cups sifted cake flour	Chocolate Fudge Frosting
2 teaspoons baking powder	(recipe follows)

Melt the chocolate in a small skillet over very low heat. Cool slightly.

Cream the butter well. Gradually add the sugar and beat until fluffy. Blend in the cooled, melted chocolate.

Add the eggs one at a time, beating well after each addition.

Sift the flour, baking powder, and salt together. Stir the vanilla into the milk and add to the creamed mixture alternately with the dry ingredients, beginning and ending with the dry ingredients. Stir well after each addition to form a smooth mixture. Stir in the nuts.

Pour the batter into two greased and floured 8-inch-square baking pans. Bake in a 350° oven for 35 to 40 minutes.

Let cool in the pans for 10 minutes, then turn out and finish cooling. Spread the Chocolate Fudge Frosting between the layers and on the top and sides. Garnish the top with additional nuts if desired.

Chocolate Fudge Frosting

½ cup butter	½ teaspoon salt
2 1-ounce squares	3 cups sifted confectioners'
unsweetened chocolate	sugar (about)
2 eggs	1 cup chopped pecans or
2 teaspoons vanilla	English walnuts

Combine the butter and chocolate in a small saucepan. Place over low heat until melted. Remove from the heat and cool slightly.

Beat the eggs slightly. Gradually pour the chocolate mixture into the eggs, beating constantly. Stir in the vanilla and salt.

Gradually stir in the confectioners' sugar and beat until smooth and of spreading consistency, adding a little more sugar if necessary. Stir in the nuts.

CRAZY CAKE

A chocolate cake batter prepared in the pan it is to be baked in. No eggs are required. Other oddities: vegetable oil, vinegar, and water.

1½ cups sifted all-purpose flour	6 tablespoons vegetable oil
1 cup sugar	1 tablespoon vinegar
3 tablespoons cocoa	1 teaspoon vanilla
1 teaspoon soda	1 cup cold water
½ teaspoon salt	Cocoa Icing (recipe follows)

Sift the flour, sugar, cocoa, soda, and salt together into an ungreased 8-inch-square baking pan.

Make 3 wells in the dry mixture with a spoon: one large, one medium, and one small. Into the large well pour the vegetable oil; into the medium well, the vinegar; into the small one, the vanilla.

Pour the cup of cold water over all. Stir with a fork until smooth; do not beat.

Bake in a 350° oven for 30 to 35 minutes. Remove from the oven and spread the Cocoa Icing evenly over the top while the cake is hot. Cool in the pan.

Cocoa Icing

3 tablespoons butter	3 tablespoons cocoa
1 cup sifted confectioners' sugar	½ teaspoon salt
	1 teaspoon vanilla

Melt the butter in a saucepan. Add the sugar, cocoa, salt, and vanilla and stir until smooth. (If too thick to spread, add a few drops of hot water.)

DEVIL'S FOOD CAKE

Preparing a chocolate-flavored custard before combining with the remaining batter ingredients is an old-time method used for Devil's Food Cake. The cake is moist and dark.

1¾ cups sugar	1 teaspoon soda
¾ cup cocoa	1 tablespoon hot water
½ teaspoon salt	2 cups sifted cake flour
3 eggs	1 teaspoon vanilla
1 cup milk	Seven-Minute Frosting
½ cup vegetable shortening	(recipe follows)

Combine ¾ cup of the sugar, the cocoa, and the salt in a saucepan. Blend in 1 egg and ½ cup of the milk. Cook, stirring over low heat until the mixture thickens slightly and will coat a clean spoon. (Do not allow it to boil.) Set aside to cool.

Cream the shortening with the remaining cup of sugar until light and fluffy. Add the remaining 2 eggs one at a time, beating well after each addition. Dissolve the soda in the hot water, then stir into the remaining ½ cup of milk.

Add the flour and the liquid ingredients alternately, beating only until blended. Add the cocoa mixture and the vanilla, beating only long enough to blend.

Spread the batter into two 9x1½-inch round layer cake pans that have been greased and floured. Bake at 350° for 30 to 35 minutes, or until the centers spring back when lightly pressed. (The batter will rise slightly above the rim of the pans, but will settle as the cake cools.)

Cool in the pans on a rack for 10 minutes, then loosen the edges and turn out. Finish cooling on the racks.

Fill and frost the top and sides with Seven-Minute Frosting, pulling the frosting up in irregular peaks.

Seven-Minute Frosting

2 egg whites	1 tablespoon light corn syrup
1½ cups sugar	½ teaspoon salt
⅓ cup water	1 teaspoon vanilla

Combine the egg whites, sugar, water, corn syrup, and salt in the top of a double boiler.

Place over rapidly boiling water and beat with an electric mixer set at medium speed, or with a rotary hand beater, until the mixture stands in peaks.

Remove from the boiling water, add the vanilla, and continue beating until the mixture forms stiff, glossy peaks.

Note: This frosting forms a crusty surface; if not desired, use ½ cup of water.

EGGLESS, MILKLESS, BUTTERLESS CAKE

Introduced in 1914, this cake was first known as War Cake, later Depression Cake. The recipe makes a large raisin spice cake that will keep well for weeks. It is served without frosting.

1 pound brown sugar	2 teaspoons cinnamon
2 cups water	1 teaspoon cloves
⅓ cup lard or other shortening	3½ cups sifted all-purpose flour
1 teaspoon salt	2 teaspoons soda
2 cups seedless raisins	¼ cup hot coffee

Combine the brown sugar, water, shortening, salt, raisins, cinnamon, and cloves in a large saucepan. Bring to a boil, stirring until the sugar is dissolved; then boil for 5 minutes without stirring. Cool in the saucepan.

Gradually stir the cooled raisin mixture into the flour. Dissolve the soda in the coffee and add, then beat the mixture well.

Turn into a well-greased and floured 13x9x2-inch baking pan. Bake at 325° for 45 to 50 minutes, or until the top springs back when lightly touched.

Cool in the pan. Serve plain.

MIDNIGHT MAYONNAISE CAKE

This easy, delicious cake is moist and black and, curiously, contains mayonnaise. The frosting is uncooked and similar to Seven-Minute Frosting, but it is as quickly made as the cake.

2 cups sifted cake flour	1 cup mayonnaise
1 cup sugar	1 cup cold water
½ cup cocoa	1 teaspoon vanilla
2 teaspoons soda	Meringue Frosting (recipe
¼ teaspoon salt	follows)

Sift the flour, sugar, cocoa, soda, and salt into a mixing bowl.

Stir in the mayonnaise, water, and vanilla. When well combined, beat well by hand for 200 strokes, scraping the spoon and bowl several times.

Pour into two greased and floured 8-inch round layer cake pans. Bake in a 350° oven for about 30 minutes.

Cool on a rack in the pans for 5 minutes, then turn out and cool completely.

Fill and frost with Meringue Frosting.

Note: Although the cake is moist and may be made a day in advance, the frosting should be prepared the same day the cake is served.

Meringue Frosting

1 egg white (at room	⅛ teaspoon salt
temperature)	1 teaspoon vanilla
¾ cup superfine sugar	¼ cup boiling water
¼ teaspoon cream of tartar	

Combine the egg white, sugar, cream of tartar, salt, and vanilla in a large mixing bowl. Beat slowly with an electric mixer (essential in this recipe) until well mixed.

Turn the mixer to high and gradually pour in the boiling water. Beat until the egg white forms stiff peaks and the sugar is completely dissolved (test with your fingers).

Note: Surprisingly, the single egg white whips into 3 cups of frosting, a generous amount to fill and frost the cake. It will not whip to full volume unless it is at room temperature and the bowl is free

from any traces of fat. To be certain, pour a teaspoon of vinegar into
the bowl and rub over the insides with paper toweling before adding
the ingredients.

OATMEAL CAKE

This chewy cake is made with rolled oats. It has a delicious topping of
butter, brown sugar, nuts, and coconut that is spread on the baked
cake, then broiled until bubbly.

1¼ cups boiling water	1 teaspoon cinnamon
1 cup quick-cooking rolled oats	1 teaspoon nutmeg
½ cup shortening	½ teaspoon salt
1 cup light brown sugar (packed)	**BROILER TOPPING**
1 cup sugar	4 tablespoons melted butter
2 eggs	½ cup light brown sugar (packed)
1⅓ cups sifted all-purpose flour	⅓ cup chopped pecans
1 teaspoon soda	½ cup shredded coconut
	2 tablespoons milk

Pour the boiling water over the rolled oats. Let stand for 20
minutes.

Cream the shortening and sugars. Add the eggs one at a time,
beating well after each addition.

Sift together the flour, soda, cinnamon, nutmeg, and salt. Add to
the creamed mixture, beating only until well blended.

Blend in the softened oats.

Pour into a greased and floured 9-inch-square baking pan. Bake
at 350° for 45 to 55 minutes.

Remove from the oven and set on a rack while preparing the
Broiler Topping.

Combine the melted butter, brown sugar, nuts, coconut, and
milk. Carefully spread over the hot cake.

Then place the cake in the broiler and broil until bubbly. Watch
carefully to avoid burning.

Remove and cool in the pan.

CHOCOLATE YEAST CAKE

High and firm-textured, this cake is similar to pound cake. The batter is made with yeast, often used as a leavener for cake batters before the invention of baking powder. The batter is mixed one day, refrigerated, and baked the next.

1 cup (½ pound) butter	1 cup milk
2 cups sugar	2¾ cups sifted cake flour
3 eggs	½ teaspoon salt
3 1-ounce squares	1 teaspoon soda
unsweetened chocolate,	3 tablespoons hot water
melted	1 teaspoon vanilla
½ cake yeast or ½ package	½ teaspoon almond extract
(1½ teaspoons) dry yeast	Chocolate Butter Frosting
¼ cup lukewarm water	(recipe follows)

Cream the butter well. Gradually beat in the sugar. Add the eggs one at a time and beat until very light. Blend in the cooled melted chocolate.

Dissolve the yeast in the lukewarm water, then stir into the milk.

Sift the flour with the salt 3 times. Add alternately to the creamed mixture with the milk mixture, beating only until blended. Cover the bowl and refrigerate overnight.

In the morning, dissolve the soda in the hot water. Stir into the cold cake batter along with the flavorings. Blend thoroughly.

Pour the cold batter into a well-greased and floured 10-inch tube pan. Bake in a 350° oven for 65 to 75 minutes, or until the cake springs back to the touch and a wooden pick comes out clean.

Cool for 15 minutes on a rack (do not invert), then remove from the pan. Invert onto the rack, cover lightly with a cloth towel to prevent excess drying, and cool completely.

Frost with Chocolate Butter Frosting, or serve unfrosted with vanilla ice cream.

Chocolate Butter Frosting

6 tablespoons butter	2 cups sifted confectioners'
4 1-ounce squares	sugar
unsweetened chocolate	⅛ teaspoon salt

| 4 tablespoons milk (about) | 1 teaspoon vanilla |
| 2 eggs | |

Melt the butter and chocolate in a saucepan over very low heat. Cool.

Combine the sugar, salt, milk, eggs, and vanilla in a chilled mixing bowl. Do not beat.

Add the cooled chocolate mixture. Beat with an electric mixer set at high speed until the frosting changes color and is of spreading consistency. If too thick, add a little more milk.

Many ranges now have oven controls, so all one has to do is to set the heat regulator at the temperature desired and the stove produces it.

It may be set for "cool," "medium" or "hot," or even to the exact degree of temperature specified in the recipe, vastly simplifying cooking.

For stoves without this control there are portable thermometers, to be placed on the oven shelf, which register the oven temperature.

—The Menu Book of the American Housewife
(1929)

CHOCOLATE CUPCAKES

Velvety cake with thick, rich chocolate frosting. The two belong together; don't make one without the other.

2 1-ounce squares unsweetened chocolate	1 cup sifted all-purpose flour
¼ cup vegetable shortening	1 teaspoon baking powder
1 cup sugar	⅛ teaspoon salt
2 eggs	½ cup milk
1 teaspoon vanilla	Glossy Chocolate Frosting (recipe follows)

Melt the chocolate over very low heat; cool.

Cream the shortening and the sugar. Add the eggs one at a time and beat until light. Stir in the chocolate and vanilla.

Sift the flour with the baking powder and salt. Add to the chocolate mixture alternately with the milk.

Spoon the batter into cupcake pans lined with paper liners. (The batter will fill 18 liners.)

Bake at 375° for 15 to 18 minutes, or until the cupcakes test done with a wooden pick.

Let cool for 5 minutes, then remove from the pans and cool completely. Frost the tops with Glossy Chocolate Frosting, swirling them attractively.

Glossy Chocolate Frosting

1 tablespoon butter	1½ cups sifted confectioners' sugar
2 tablespoons vegetable shortening	¼ teaspoon salt (scant)
3 1-ounce squares unsweetened chocolate	¼ cup hot milk
	½ teaspoon vanilla

Melt the shortenings and the chocolate together in a saucepan set over low heat. Stir to blend.

Combine the sugar and salt in a bowl. Add the hot milk, stirring until the sugar is dissolved. Blend in the vanilla and the chocolate mixture. Beat with a spoon until smooth and thick enough to spread.

Note: This will frost the 18 cupcakes generously.

GINGERBREAD

Soft gingerbread is an early New England invention. The European varieties that preceded this type were hard and thin. For the first hundred years it was considered a hot bread to be served spread with butter, not as a dessert, and was spiced only with ginger. The one presented adds cinnamon and cloves. It is rich and moist.

½ cup shortening
½ cup sugar
2 eggs
1 cup black New Orleans molasses
1 cup boiling water
2½ cups sifted all-purpose flour

2 teaspoons soda
1 teaspoon ginger
1 teaspoon cinnamon
½ teaspoon cloves
½ teaspoon salt
Butter or whipped cream

Cream the shortening and sugar. Add the eggs and mix thoroughly. Blend in the molasses and boiling water.

Sift together the flour, soda, ginger, cinnamon, cloves, and salt. Add to the molasses mixture and beat until smooth.

Pour into a well-greased and floured 9-inch-square baking pan. Bake at 325° for 40 to 45 minutes.

Cut into squares and serve hot with butter or whipped cream.

Nutmeg, Cinnamon, Cloves, Mace, and Allspice should be pounded fine, and corked tight in small glass bottles, with mouths large enough for a junk-bottle cork, and then put in a tight tin box, made for the purpose. Or they can be put in small tin boxes with tight covers. Essences are as good as spices.

—Miss Beecher's Housekeeper and Healthkeeper
by Catharine E. Beecher (1873)

PUMPKIN SPICE CAKE

Fluffy, with a deep golden color.

2¼ cups sifted cake flour
½ teaspoon salt
3 teaspoons baking powder
½ teaspoon soda
½ teaspoon cinnamon
½ teaspoon nutmeg
¾ cup milk

1 cup canned pumpkin
½ cup vegetable shortening
1¼ cups sugar
2 eggs
Whipped Cream Filling and
Frosting (recipe follows)

Sift the flour, salt, baking powder, soda, cinnamon, and nutmeg together 3 times. Set aside.

Gradually blend the milk into the pumpkin. Set aside.

Cream the shortening and sugar until light and fluffy. Add the eggs one at a time, beating well after each addition.

Add the flour mixture alternately with the pumpkin mixture, beating just until blended after each addition.

Spread the batter evenly in two well-greased 8-inch layer cake pans, making the sides slightly higher than the center.

Bake at 350° for 30 to 35 minutes, or until the centers spring back lightly to the touch. Cool on racks for 10 minutes, then turn out and cool completely. Fill and frost with Whipped Cream Filling and Frosting.

Whipped Cream Filling and Frosting

1 teaspoon unflavored gelatin
2 tablespoons cold water
2 tablespoons hot water

2 cups heavy cream
½ cup confectioners' sugar
1 teaspoon cinnamon

Sprinkle the gelatin over the cold water in a cup. Let stand until softened, then add the hot water, stirring until dissolved.

Beat the cream until it begins to thicken slightly. Gradually add the confectioners' sugar and cinnamon and continue beating until the cream begins to hold its shape. Beat in the dissolved gelatin a little at a time and continue beating until stiff enough to spread, but not buttery.

TOMATO SOUP CAKE

An unusual spice cake made with canned tomato soup. Surprisingly, cakes calling for this ingredient have been in existence for at least 50 years.

2 cups sifted cake flour
3 teaspoons baking powder
½ teaspoon soda
½ teaspoon cloves
½ teaspoon cinnamon
½ teaspoon nutmeg
1 cup seedless raisins

½ cup vegetable shortening
1 cup sugar
2 eggs
1 can (1¼ cups) condensed tomato soup
Cream Cheese Frosting (recipe follows)

Sift together the flour, baking powder, soda, cloves, cinnamon, and nutmeg.

Rinse the raisins and roll in a small amount of the flour mixture. (If the raisins are cut in half, the cake will be easier to cut.)

Cream the shortening with the sugar. Add the eggs one at a time, beating well.

Add the flour mixture alternately with the tomato soup, then stir until smooth. Fold in the floured raisins.

Pour into two greased and floured 8-inch round layer cake pans. Bake in a 375° oven for 30 to 35 minutes. Cool, then fill and frost with Cream Cheese Frosting.

Cream Cheese Frosting

1 3-ounce package cream cheese
2 tablespoons butter
2 cups sifted confectioners' sugar

½ teaspoon vanilla
Light cream

Soften the cream cheese and butter to room temperature. Gradually stir in the sugar and beat until smooth. Blend in the vanilla and enough cream to make it the proper consistency for spreading.

PRUNE CAKE

A moist spice cake with a filling containing chopped prunes and a frosting made with whipped cream.

¾ cup vegetable shortening	½ teaspoon salt
1 cup sugar	1 teaspoon cinnamon
3 egg yolks	1 teaspoon allspice
3 tablespoons buttermilk	3 egg whites
1 cup finely chopped cooked prunes*	Prune Filling (recipe follows)
2 cups sifted cake flour	Whipped Cream Frosting (recipe follows)
1 teaspoon soda	

Cream the shortening with the sugar until fluffy. Add the egg yolks one at a time and beat until creamy.

Stir in the buttermilk and prunes.

Sift the flour with the soda, salt, cinnamon, and allspice 3 times. Add to the creamed mixture and beat until smooth.

Beat the egg whites until stiff but still moist. Stir in one-half of the egg whites to lighten the batter, then fold in the remainder.

Turn into two greased and floured 9-inch layer cake pans. Bake at 350° for 30 to 35 minutes.

Cool in the pans on racks for 10 minutes, then remove and cool completely.

Fill with Prune Filling and frost the sides and top with Whipped Cream Frosting. Chill for 2 or 3 hours before serving. (The gelatin gives body to the whipped cream; it will hold for a day or two without seeping into the cake.)

Prune Filling

1 cup sugar	1 tablespoon butter
¼ teaspoon salt	½ teaspoon vanilla
2 eggs	
½ cup finely chopped cooked prunes*	

Combine the sugar, salt, and eggs in a saucepan. Beat until smooth. Stir in the chopped prunes. Cook, stirring constantly until the mixture thickens slightly. (Do not boil.)

*Packaged prunes labeled "ready to eat" may be used without cooking.

Remove from the heat and stir in the butter and vanilla. Cool.

Whipped Cream Frosting

¾ teaspoon unflavored gelatin
1 tablespoon cold water
2 tablespoons hot water

¾ teaspoon lemon juice
1½ cups heavy cream
⅓ cup confectioners' sugar

Sprinkle the gelatin over the cold water in a cup. Let stand until softened, then add the hot water and lemon juice and stir until dissolved.

Beat the cream with the confectioners' sugar until it begins to hold its shape, then gradually beat in the dissolved gelatin. Continue beating until stiff but not buttery.

RAW APPLE CAKE

This moist apple cake cuts better the second day and will keep for at least a week.

½ cup butter
½ cup light brown sugar
   (packed)
1 cup sugar
2 eggs
1 teaspoon lemon juice
1 teaspoon grated lemon rind
2¼ cups sifted all-purpose
   flour
1 teaspoon baking powder

1 teaspoon salt
1 teaspoon soda
1 cup milk
2 cups peeled chopped
   apples

TOPPING
2 tablespoons sugar
½ cup chopped pecans

Cream the butter. Gradually add the sugars, then beat well. Add the eggs one at a time, beating well after each addition. Add the lemon juice and rind.

Sift the flour with the baking powder and salt. Dissolve the soda in the milk. Add the dry ingredients and milk alternately to the first mixture, beginning and ending with the flour.

Fold in the chopped apples.

Pour into a greased and floured 13x9-inch baking pan. Sprinkle the 2 tablespoons of sugar and the pecans evenly over the top.

Bake in a 350° oven for 45 to 50 minutes. Test with a wooden pick. Cool and store in the pan.

GLAZED ORANGE CAKE

Sweetened orange juice is poured over the warm cake to make a glaze.

½ cup butter
1 cup sugar
2 eggs
1 cup raisins
Grated rind of 1 orange
2 cups sifted all-purpose
flour
1 teaspoon baking powder
1 teaspoon soda

¼ teaspoon salt
1 cup sour milk or
buttermilk

GLAZE
½ cup sugar
Juice of 1 orange (6
tablespoons)

Cream the butter well. Gradually add the sugar and beat until light and fluffy. Add the eggs one at a time, beating well after each addition. Continue beating until light.

Chop the raisins in a food grinder or a food processor. Grate the rind of the orange, trimming off only the zest (not the spongy white part). Stir the raisins and zest into the egg mixture.

Sift the flour, baking powder, soda, and salt together. Add alternately with the milk in thirds, beginning and ending with the flour. Beat only until blended.

Pour into a greased and floured 13x9-inch baking pan and spread evenly. Bake in a 325° oven for 35 to 45 minutes, or until the center springs back to the touch.

While the cake is baking, prepare the Glaze. Stir the sugar into the orange juice until it is dissolved.

When the cake is removed from the oven, dribble the glaze mixture over the hot cake, spreading with the back of a spoon to cover evenly.

Cool the cake on a rack, then cover and store in the baking pan until ready to serve. Serve plain or with whipped cream.

Note: This cake is best served a day after baking. It keeps well.

What's in a name?
This delicious two-layer pie,
called Montgomery Pie
by the Pennsylvania Dutch (page 168),
is more descriptively known
as Lemon Sponge Pie or Lemon Cake Pie.

PINEAPPLE CAKE

A quickly mixed loaf cake. The ingredients are dumped into a bowl and beaten by hand until well-blended. The warm cake is frosted with a buttery cream cheese frosting. It is best refrigerated overnight before eating. This cake will keep well for at least a week.

1 No. 2 can crushed
    pineapple (2⅓ cups with
    juice)
2 cups sugar
2 eggs
2 cups sifted all-purpose
    flour

2 teaspoons soda
½ teaspoon salt
1 teaspoon vanilla
1 cup chopped walnuts
    Cream Cheese Frosting
    (recipe follows)

Pour the pineapple into a mixing bowl. Add the sugar, eggs, flour, soda, salt, vanilla, and walnuts.

Beat by hand until well blended (about 2 minutes).

Pour into a well-greased and floured 13x9x2-inch pan. Bake at 350° for 40 to 45 minutes.

Cool on a rack in the pan until slightly warm, then spread the top with the Cream Cheese Frosting. Refrigerate for at least 24 hours before serving.

Cream Cheese Frosting

1 8-ounce package cream
    cheese
½ cup margarine

1⅓ cups sifted confectioners'
    sugar
1 teaspoon vanilla

Soften the cream cheese and margarine to room temperature. Cream together, then blend in the sugar and vanilla. Spread over the warm cake.

Extracts for cake are better and stronger and take less if dropped on top of the cake after it is baked.
            —Mrs. Owens' Cook Book and Useful Household Hints
                by Frances E. Owens, 1888 Revised Edition (1884)

FRESH BLUEBERRY CAKE

Delicious served cold from the refrigerator.

1 egg
⅔ cup sugar
1½ cups plus 2 teaspoons sifted
    cake flour
2 teaspoons baking powder
½ teaspoon salt
⅓ cup milk
3 tablespoons melted butter

1 teaspoon vanilla
⅛ teaspoon almond extract
1½ cups fresh blueberries

TOPPING
1 tablespoon sugar
Whipped cream (optional)

Beat the egg slightly. Gradually beat in the sugar and continue beating until light.

Sift the 1½ cups of flour, the baking powder, and the salt together. Add alternately with the milk, beginning and ending with the flour.

Blend in the melted butter and flavorings.

Sprinkle the 2 teaspoons of flour over the blueberries, then fold them into the batter.

Pour into a greased and floured 8-inch-square cake pan. Sprinkle the top with the tablespoon of sugar. Bake at 400° for 30 minutes. Test with a wooden pick.

Cool on a rack in the pan. When cool, cover and refrigerate. Cut the cake into squares and serve plain or with whipped cream.

BANANA CAKE

2¼ cups sifted cake flour
¾ teaspoon baking powder
½ teaspoon soda
½ teaspoon salt
½ cup butter
1½ cups sugar
2 teaspoons vanilla

1 cup (2 to 3) mashed ripe
bananas
3 egg yolks
¼ cup buttermilk
3 egg whites
Caramel Frosting (recipe
follows)

Sift the flour, baking powder, soda, and salt together 3 times.

Cream the butter with 1¼ cups of the sugar and the vanilla until light and fluffy. Blend in the mashed bananas.

Add the egg yolks one at a time, beating well after each addition.

Add the flour mixture alternately with the buttermilk, beginning and ending with the flour.

Beat the egg whites until soft peaks form. Gradually beat in the remaining ¼ cup of sugar and continue beating until they are stiff. Fold them into the batter.

Turn into two greased and floured 9-inch layer cake pans. Bake at 350° for 25 to 30 minutes.

Cool on racks for 10 minutes, then turn out and cool completely. Fill and frost the layers with Caramel Frosting.

Caramel Frosting

2 cups dark brown sugar
3 tablespoons butter
3 tablespoons vegetable
shortening

½ cup milk
2 cups sifted confectioners'
sugar
Cream

Combine the brown sugar, butter, shortening, and milk in a heavy saucepan. Cook, stirring over low heat until the sugar is melted. Bring to a boil and let boil without stirring for 5 minutes.

Remove from the heat and let the mixture stand until lukewarm. Beat in the confectioners' sugar, then beat in just enough cream (a few teaspoons) to make the frosting of spreading consistency and give it a gloss.

JAM CAKE

Although jam cakes were prized by pioneer women for their keeping quality, we are indebted to the Southern states, particularly Kentucky, for preserving the recipes for posterity. Old-time versions were simple mixtures containing homemade jam and spices. Updated versions may include a variety of preserved fruits in addition. Like fruitcake, it is served during the holidays. Although any jam can be used, blackberry remains a favorite.

3 cups sifted cake flour
1½ teaspoons soda
1½ teaspoons salt
1 teaspoon cinnamon
1 teaspoon cloves
½ teaspoon nutmeg
½ teaspoon allspice
¾ cup vegetable shortening

1⅓ cups light brown sugar (packed)
3 eggs
1 cup sour milk or buttermilk
1 cup seedless blackberry jam
Caramel Frosting (recipe follows)

Sift together the flour, soda, salt, and spices 3 times.

Cream the shortening and brown sugar, beating until light and fluffy. Add the eggs one at a time, beating well after each addition.

Add the sifted dry ingredients alternately with the milk, beginning and ending with the flour. Fold in the jam, mixing only until well blended.

Turn the batter into three greased and floured 9-inch round layer cake pans. Bake in a 350° oven for 30 to 35 minutes.

Cool on racks for 10 minutes, then turn out and cool completely. Fill and frost with Caramel Frosting.

Caramel Frosting

¾ cup (1½ sticks) butter
1½ cups light brown sugar (packed)
¼ teaspoon salt

6 tablespoons milk
1 teaspoon vanilla
3 cups sifted confectioners' sugar (about)

Melt the butter in a saucepan. Stir in the brown sugar and salt. Cook over low heat, stirring constantly for 2 minutes. Add the milk, stirring until the mixture comes to a boil. Remove from the heat and cool to lukewarm.

Stir in the vanilla, then gradually blend in the confectioners' sugar, stirring and adding sugar until it is thick enough to spread.

WHITE FRUITCAKE

This fruitcake contains fresh coconut.

1 pound golden raisins
½ pound whole candied
    cherries
¼ pound diced candied citron
¼ pound diced candied
    orange peel
3 cups grated fresh coconut
    (loosely packed)*

¾ cup (1½ sticks) butter
2 cups sugar
3½ cups sifted all-purpose
    flour
1 cup water
2 teaspoons lemon extract
6 egg whites

Combine the raisins, cherries, citron, orange peel, and coconut; set aside.

Beat the butter with the sugar until light and fluffy. Add the flour alternately with the combined water and lemon extract. Blend well.

Stir in the fruits.

Beat the egg whites until they form stiff, moist points. Fold about one-fourth of the egg whites into the batter, then fold in the remainder.

Grease a 9- or 10-inch tube pan. Line the bottom and sides with heavy brown paper, cut to fit, and grease the paper.

Turn the batter into the pan. Bake in a 250° oven for 3 hours to 3 hours and 15 minutes.

Let cool on a rack for 1 hour, then remove from the pan and cool completely. Wrap with plastic wrap, then with foil. Store in the refrigerator. It will keep well for a month or two.

*See page 95 for the method of preparing grated fresh coconut.

BLACK FRUITCAKE

In Martha Washington's day, fruitcakes were called "great cakes." They were featured at Mount Vernon on Christmas, Twelfth Night, and on other "great days."

½ pound (2 cups) shelled pecans
¼ pound (¾ cup) candied lemon peel
¼ pound (¾ cup) candied orange peel
½ pound (1½ cups) candied citron
¾ pound (2¼ cups) candied cherries
¾ pound (2¼ cups) candied pineapple
1 pound (3¼ cups) currants
½ pound (1 rounded cup) dates
½ pound (1 rounded cup) dried uncooked prunes

1 cup black New Orleans molasses
1 cup honey
½ cup cider
1 pound (2 cups) butter
1 pound (2¼ cups packed) brown sugar
10 eggs
1 pound (4 cups sifted) all-purpose flour
1 teaspoon baking powder
1 teaspoon cinnamon
½ teaspoon cloves
½ teaspoon allspice

Break the pecans into pieces. Unless the candied peels are very small, cut them thinner. Cut the cherries into halves. Cut the pineapple into small pieces if necessary. Snip the dates and prunes into small pieces.

Combine the fruits and nuts. Stir in the molasses, honey, and cider. Cover and let stand overnight.

Cream the butter. Gradually add the brown sugar and beat until light. Add 4 of the eggs, one by one, beating well after each addition.

Sift the flour with the baking powder, cinnamon, cloves, and allspice. Add one-third of the flour mixture to the batter and beat well. Add another third and beat well again.

Beat in the remaining 6 eggs, one at a time. Fold in the fruits and liquid, then gradually blend in the remaining flour mixture.

Grease three 10x5x3-inch loaf pans. Line the bottoms and sides with heavy paper or a double layer of waxed paper and grease the paper.

Turn the batter into the prepared pans (they should be only two-thirds full).

Bake in a 250° oven for 2½ hours, then increase the heat to 275° and bake 45 minutes to 1 hour longer.

Cool on racks for 30 minutes. Run a knife around the edges while they are still warm, then invert on racks to cool completely.

Wrap the cakes in a cloth dampened with cider. Cover with foil and store in a dry place.

After a week sprinkle the tops with a tablespoon of cider, bourbon, or rum. Repeat each week for several weeks. If held for months, moisten every 2 or 3 months.

TO ICE A GREAT CAKE

Take the Whites of twenty-four Eggs, and a Pound of double-refin'd Sugar beat and sifted fine, mix both together in a deep earthen Pan, and with a Wisk wisk it well for two or three hours together till it looks white and thick, then with a thin broad Board or Bunch of Feathers spread it all over the Top and Sides of the Cake; set it at a proper Distance before a good clear Fire, and keep turning it continually for fear of its changing Colour; but a cool Oven is best, and an Hour will harden it. You may perfume the Icing with what Perfume you please.

—The Art of Cookery Made Plain and Easy
by Mrs. [Hannah] Glasse (1751)

KENTUCKY WHISKEY CAKE

Old-time fruitcakes were often based on standard pound cake recipes with preserved fruits and nuts added. This famous Southern cake is an example.

1½ pounds (6 cups) shelled pecans	2 whole nutmegs
1 pound (3 cups) seedless raisins	1 cup bourbon whiskey
1 pound (4 cups sifted) all-purpose flour	½ pound butter
2 teaspoons baking powder	1 pound (2¼ cups packed) light brown sugar
	6 egg yolks
	6 egg whites

Break the pecans into pieces or chop coarsely. Cut the raisins in half.

Sift the flour. Remove 2 tablespoons and mix with the nuts and raisins. Sift the remaining flour with the baking powder.

Grate the nutmegs into the whiskey and let stand for at least 10 minutes.

Cream the butter and brown sugar until light. Add the egg yolks one at a time, beating until the mixture is smooth and lemon-colored and forms a ribbon on the batter when the beaters are raised.

Add the flour mixture and the whiskey mixture alternately to the egg mixture, beating only until blended.

Gradually fold in the pecans and raisins.

Beat the egg whites until stiff. Stir about ¼ of the egg whites into the batter to lighten it, then fold in the remainder.

Grease a 9- or 10-inch tube pan. Line the bottom and sides with heavy brown paper, cut to fit, and grease the paper. Pour in the batter and let stand for 10 minutes to settle. Then bake in a 275° oven for about 3 hours or until a cake tester comes out clean.

Remove from the oven and place on a rack to cool for 2 hours before removing from the pan.

Wrap and store in a cold place, or refrigerate, for at least a week before serving. It will keep indefinitely.

Slice while cold to prevent crumbling. The slices will quickly come to room temperature for serving.

IV

Pies

The pie is an English institution, which when planted in American soil, forthwith ran rampant and burst forth an untold variety of genera and species.
—HARRIET BEECHER STOWE

Befitting their life-style, early New England settlers constructed their pies from the ingredients at hand. Pumpkin pies emerged from English custards. Cranberries and other berries that grew wild were important ingredients. So were apples, which in the first few years had to be imported.

As the settlers gained control of their environment and planted orchards and gardens, the variety of their pies expanded to include pieplant (rhubarb), tomatoes, peaches, and grapes.

Pies were so popular that they were eaten twice a day, including breakfast. Often fillings were prepared in quantity and preserved; in winter, pies were made by the dozens and frozen.

Prior to the Revolutionary War, fruit pies were baked in deep dishes without a top crust. The hardships of the war led cooks to bake their pies in shallow pans and cover them with pastry crusts in order to stretch the fillings and satisfy more diners. Necessity became the mother of an invention that is now the standard double-crust fruit pie, which is distinctly American.

Until the turn of the nineteenth century, the fillings constituted one-third of the thickness of the pie and the crusts the other two-thirds. Until the 1930s the standard pastry crust was made with butter or lard. After the introduction of vegetable shortening at that time, the standard became the crust made from this product.

Pies made with one-crust soft fillings were thought of as puddings and were often listed as such in cookbooks as late as the middle of the nineteenth century.

As the popularity of the single-crust pie grew, many regional specialties developed. Among the best of these are the Pennsylvania

Dutch Apple Crumb Pie, the molasses-flavored Shoofly Pie, the Transparent Pies of the South, and the Key Lime Pie of Florida.

The chiffon pie, a more recent (1921) addition, was made with whipped egg whites set in a graham cracker crust. Eventually, the chiffon pie was made with gelatin and became the first of a series of American refrigerator pies containing gelatin.

Pastry and Pie Fillings

In general, the recipes for pies, and the following section on pastry, provide sufficient information for successful pie making and baking. There are a few points, however, that should be made clear.

1. Standard-size 8- or 9-inch pie plates should be used. Glass heatproof plates are preferable, since the undercrust will brown quickly and help prevent the filling from soaking in during baking. (Beware of substituting frozen pie crusts: the pans are smaller and are made of shiny aluminum, which causes soaking.)

2. The proper pastry recipe or method of mixing should be chosen according to the filling used. (See the recipes for pastry that follow.) For pies with thin unbaked fillings, additional precaution should be taken to prevent the filling from seeping into the crust. Chill the pastry shell before filling, partially bake it, or brush it with a little egg white or whole egg and allow this to dry before filling.

3. Most pies should be baked on a rack set in the middle of the oven. Juicy berry pies are an exception; they should be baked on the lowest rack (and at a high temperature, at least during the first part of baking) to set the crust before the juices can seep into it.

4. Baked pies should be cooled on a rack to prevent sweating, which causes the undercrust to become soggy.

5. Leftover cream, custard, or chiffon pies should be refrigerated to prevent the growth of harmful bacteria. Fruit pies may be stored at room temperature, then freshened by reheating for a few minutes in a warm oven.

6. When whipped cream is used as a topping for a chilled pie filling, the filling should be thoroughly chilled. The cream should be whipped just until it will form moist peaks. Overbeaten cream may separate and weep onto the filling. If properly whipped, the cream will hold for several hours. As a precaution, the whipped cream may be spread over the pie filling just before serving, or passed separately.

Meringues for Pies

Although recipes for meringues are given with the individual pie recipes, to make a perfect meringue the preparation, baking, cooling, and storing require fuller explanation.

1. For highest volume, the egg whites should be at room temperature and without a trace of egg yolk.

2. The sugar should be added gradually, a tablespoon at a time, when the beaten egg whites stand in soft peaks and are losing their frothy look. In addition to beating well after each spoonful of sugar is added, the beating must be continued until the meringue is stiff and glossy and the sugar has dissolved completely. If the sugar is added too soon, or the mixture has not been beaten long enough, the meringue will not be as high and may be grainy. The undissolved sugar will also cause "beading" (droplets of syrup) on the baked meringue.

3. The meringue should be lightly browned in a 350° to 425° oven. Too high a temperature or overbaking will cause shrinkage; too low a temperature will make the meringue tough. Baked properly, the meringue will be tender and easy to cut through.

4. The meringue should be spread on a filling that has cooled slightly. If either the filling or the crust is hot, a layer of liquid may form on top of the filling. The meringue should be attached securely to the crust, with no filling showing, to prevent shrinking and to insulate the filling during the baking.

5. To prevent the meringue from falling during cooling, it should be cooled slowly away from drafts, then stored in a cool place or refrigerated. If refrigerated before cooling, both the filling and meringue may weep.

6. To cut through a meringue easily, a knife should first be dipped into warm water, then dried. The process should be repeated as often as necessary so that the knife will slide through the meringue.

STANDARD PASTRY FOR DOUBLE-CRUST PIE
(8- or 9-inch)

This is the standard pastry for American pies of today. It is an all-purpose pastry that may be used for any pie requiring a pastry crust. It is crisp and flaky.

2¼ cups sifted all-purpose flour	¾ cup vegetable shortening
1⅛ teaspoons salt	5–6 tablespoons cold water

Sift the flour and salt together into a mixing bowl. Cut in half the shortening with a pastry blender until it looks like coarse meal. Cut in the remaining shortening until it is the size of large peas. Sprinkle the water over the mixture, a tablespoon at a time, mixing lightly with a fork and adding only enough water to moisten the flour.

When the dough holds together, gather it into a ball, then divide it into two balls, one slightly larger than the other. Flatten each.

Roll the larger part out on a lightly floured board into a circle ⅛ inch thick (about 1½ inches larger than an inverted 9-inch pie plate, 2 inches larger than an 8-inch pie plate).

Transfer to the pie plate and ease into shape. Trim the edges with scissors to a ½-inch overhang, then fold under.

Repeat the rolling procedure for the remaining dough, rolling a little thinner than for the bottom crust.

Prepare the filling and turn into the pastry-lined pan. Moisten the edge of the pastry with cold water. Cover with the remaining rolled pastry and trim to a ½-inch overhang, then fold under the edge of the lower pastry. Press together to seal, then flute or press the edge flat with the tines of a fork.

Cut several vents near the center to allow the steam to escape during baking. Bake as directed for the filling used.

Lattice Top: Roll out the pastry for the top crust into a rectangle ⅛ inch thick. Cut strips ⅜ inch wide with a sharp knife or a pastry wheel. Arrange one layer of strips over the filling 1 inch apart; place the second layer over the top at a 45° angle. Press around the moistened rim, then cut off the excess pastry, leaving a ½-inch overhang. Fold these strips under the lower pastry and flute or press with the tines of a fork. Bake as directed.

Glaze: Brush the pastry top with milk or cream for a dull glaze, or use half of a slightly beaten whole egg, an egg yolk blended with 2 teaspoons of water, or a slightly beaten egg white. This produces a shiny glaze.

For a sugary top, dust the glaze lightly with sugar, or sprinkle the rolled pastry top with sugar and lightly roll in before placing it over the pie.

ICING FOR TARTS

Beat the yolks of two eggs and some melted butter together, lay it over the tarts with a feather, and then sift some sugar upon them.

—Modern American Cookery
by Miss Prudence Smith (1835)

GOLDEN PASTRY FOR DOUBLE-CRUST PIE
(8- or 9-inch)

The egg and sugar provide golden color to the crust as well as added richness.

2 cups sifted all-purpose flour	¾ cup vegetable shortening
1 tablespoon sugar	1 egg yolk
1 teaspoon salt	¼ cup milk (about)
	1 tablespoon lemon juice

Sift the flour, sugar, and salt into a mixing bowl. Cut in half the shortening with a pastry blender until it looks like coarse meal; cut in the remainder until it is the size of large peas.

Beat the egg yolk slightly and stir in 3 tablespoons of the milk and the lemon juice. Sprinkle a little at a time over the flour mixture, mixing in lightly with a fork. Continue adding the remaining milk until the mixture is moistened and begins to cling together.

Gather the dough into a ball, then divide into two balls, one slightly larger than the other. Flatten each.

Note: For rolling and preparing the pastry for the pie plate, see Standard Pastry for Double-Crust Pie.

STANDARD PASTRY FOR SINGLE-CRUST PIE
(8- or 9-inch)

1 cup plus 2 tablespoons
sifted all-purpose flour
½ teaspoon salt

6 tablespoons vegetable
shortening
2½–3 tablespoons cold water

Sift the flour and salt together into a mixing bowl. Cut in half the shortening with a pastry blender until it looks like coarse meal; cut in the remainder of the shortening until it is the size of large peas.

Sprinkle the cold water over the mixture, a tablespoon at a time. Mix lightly with a fork until all the flour is moistened and the dough barely clings together.

Gather the dough into a ball, then pat flat.

Note: For custard or other pies with thin fillings, sift half the flour and salt into the bowl. Cut in all the shortening until it looks like meal; add the remaining flour and blend well. Use warm water rather than cold water (slightly less will be required). The crust will be crumbly rather than flaky, but the filling is less apt to soak into the crust during baking.

Roll the dough out on a lightly floured board ⅛ inch thick (about 1½ inches larger in diameter than an inverted 9-inch pie plate, 2 inches larger than an inverted 8-inch pie plate).

Transfer to the pie plate; trim the edges to a ½-inch overhang, then fold under and flute, or press the edge flat with the tines of a fork. Bake as directed for the filling used.

Baked Pastry Shell: Prick the pastry thoroughly with a fork to prevent puffing during baking. Bake in a 400° oven for 10 to 12 minutes, or until golden brown. Check after 5 minutes. If the pastry puffs in the center, prick again 2 or 3 times to release the air. Cool on a rack. Brush with melted butter and refrigerate to set before filling. This will help prevent a soggy crust.

The essentials to good pie-crust are good sifted flour, good butter, and sweet lard. Use very cold water for wetting, and roll the crust from you. A quick oven is necessary for almost all kinds of pies. Mince is about the only exception.

—Mrs. Owens' Cook Book and Useful Household Hints
by Frances E. Owens, 1888 Revised Edition (1884)

PASTRY WITH LARD FOR DOUBLE-CRUST PIE
(8- or 9-inch)

Many pastry bakers are convinced that the best pastry is made with lard, because it provides superior flakiness, tenderness, and flavor. This pastry is at its best when used for fruit pies that are to be served warm.

2 cups sifted all-purpose flour	4 tablespoons cold water (about)
1 teaspoon salt	
⅔ cup lard (at room temperature)	

Sift the flour and salt together into a mixing bowl. Cut the lard into the flour mixture with a pastry blender until the mixture resembles coarse meal.

Sprinkle the water a tablespoon at a time over the dry ingredients. Mix lightly with a fork, adding just enough water so that the dough holds together.

Gather the dough into a ball, then divide into two balls, one slightly larger than the other. Press flat.

Note: For rolling and preparing the dough for the pie plate, see Standard Pastry for Double-Crust Pie, page 142.

WATER-WHIP PASTRY FOR SINGLE-CRUST PIE
(8- or 9-inch)

This method produces a crumbly, rather than a flaky, crust. It is best suited for custard pies and others with thin fillings, since the liquid is less likely to seep into the crust during baking. It is simple to make and provides a generous amount of soft, pliable dough that means instant success for beginning pastry makers. The original water-whip concept called for lard. When it was reintroduced with vegetable shortening in the 1950s by a leading manufacturer, this pastry became a standard.

½ cup plus 1 tablespoon
    vegetable shortening
2 tablespoons boiling water
1½ teaspoons milk

1½ cups sifted all-purpose
    flour
¾ teaspoon salt

Measure the shortening into a mixing bowl. Pour the boiling water and milk over the top. Break up the shortening with a fork, then beat until thick like whipped cream.

Sift the flour and salt together over the shortening mixture. Stir quickly around the bowl until the mixture clings together and cleans the bowl. Shape into a flat cake.

Roll the dough ⅛ inch thick between 2 sheets of waxed paper. To allow the pastry to spread freely, it may be necessary to lift the paper and turn once or twice.

Carefully peel off the top sheet and center the pastry over the pie plate, pastry side down. Remove the paper and ease the pastry into the plate. Trim to a ¾-inch overhang, turn under and raise the fold, and make a high fluted rim. Bake as directed for the filling used.

BUTTER PASTRY FOR BAKED PIE SHELL
(8- or 9-inch)

Because it is made with butter, this pastry has added flavor. It is perfect for glazed fruit tarts or chiffon pies.

1 cup sifted all-purpose flour
1 teaspoon baking powder

1 tablespoon sugar
½ teaspoon salt

½ cup softened sweet butter*   1 tablespoon cold water

Sift the flour, baking powder, sugar, and salt together into a mixing bowl. Cut in the butter until it has the consistency of coarse meal. Add the water a few drops at a time, tossing with a fork until all the flour is moistened.

Gather the dough together and press firmly into a ball, then press into a flat cake. Wrap in waxed paper and chill for at least 15 minutes, or until firm. (If held longer, let stand at room temperature until pliable before rolling.)

Roll the chilled dough out on a lightly floured board into a circle 1½ to 2 inches larger than the inverted pie plate. The dough should be less than ⅛ inch thick.

Ease the dough into the pan and trim to a ¾-inch overhang. Turn the edge under and flute to make a stand-up collar. Chill for at least 10 minutes, or until firm.

Prick the pastry thoroughly with a fork and bake in a 400° oven for about 12 minutes, or until golden. Check after 5 minutes. If the pastry puffs in the center, prick again 2 or 3 times to release the air. Cool on a rack.

*If salted butter is used, use ¼ teaspoon salt.

GRAHAM CRACKER CRUST
(8- or 9-inch)

Said to have been invented for chiffon pies by the commercial baker who invented them.

1¼ cups graham cracker   ¼ cup sugar
    crumbs   ¼ cup melted butter

Place the graham cracker crumbs and sugar in a bowl. Add the melted butter and work with a wooden spoon to moisten the crumbs. Blend well.

Press the mixture evenly and firmly onto the bottom and sides of a pie plate.

Bake at 375° for 8 minutes. Cool.

Note: If desired, the crust may be left unbaked and chilled. Baking makes a firmer, crunchier crust.

MERINGUE CRUST FOR ANGEL PIE
(9-inch)

4 egg whites	¼ teaspoon salt
¼ teaspoon cream of tartar	1 cup sugar

Beat the egg whites until foamy, then add the cream of tartar and salt. Beat until the egg whites hold firm peaks but are not quite stiff.

Gradually beat in the sugar, a tablespoon at a time. Continue beating until the whites are glossy and very thick and the sugar is completely dissolved. (Test with your fingers.)

Note: If the sugar is added too soon, there will be less volume; if added too rapidly, the sugar will not completely dissolve and the meringue will be granular.

Spread the meringue over the bottom and sides of a well-greased 9-inch pie plate, spreading it out to, but not over, the edge. The center should be less thick than the sides to allow for the filling when baked.

Bake in a 275° oven for 1 hour, or until the meringue is barely cream-colored and is crisp.

Turn off the heat and cool for 20 minutes in the oven with the door open. Then finish cooling on a rack at room temperature away from drafts. (The meringue will crack and fall in the center as it cools.)

Pecan Meringue Crust: After the last of the sugar has been added, beat in 1 teaspoon of vanilla and continue beating until stiff. Then fold in ½ cup of finely chopped pecans.

Line soup-dishes with a light crust, double on the rim, and fill them and bake them until the crust is done. Little bars of crust, a quarter of an inch in width, crossed on top of the tart before it is baked, are ornamental.

—Miss Beecher's Housekeeper and Healthkeeper
by Catharine E. Beecher (1873)

APPLE PIE

In 1635 William Blaxton, a clergyman, is said to have planted an apple orchard in Rhode Island that produced what is now called the Rhode Island Greening. It was the first apple, as a distinct type, to be grown in the New World. Colonial cooks fashioned their pies after those of England, stewing and straining the apples first, then baking the sauce in a crust. In the 1880s sliced apples were often baked in a crust until tender, the top crust raised and the sugar and seasonings added at the very end. Cookbooks from that century claim that this method required less sugar. To ease in the removal of the top crust, the edges were first spread with butter.

Pastry for an 8-inch double-crust pie (page 142)
4 cups (1½ pounds) tart apples,* sliced ⅓ inch thick
¼ cup light brown sugar (packed)
½ cup sugar
1 tablespoon plus 1 teaspoon flour
¾ teaspoon cinnamon
⅛ teaspoon freshly grated nutmeg (scant)
¼ teaspoon salt
2 tablespoons butter
Cheddar cheese or ice cream

Line the pie plate with pastry; trim it. Arrange half the apple slices in the pastry shell.

Combine the sugars, flour, cinnamon, nutmeg, and salt. Sprinkle half over the apples in the shell. Fill the shell with the rest of the apples, heaping them in the center. Sprinkle the remaining dry ingredients over the top. Dot with the butter.

Fit the top crust over the top. Trim; wet the bottom edge, seal, and flute. Cut several slits about an inch from the center to allow the steam to escape.

Bake at 425° for 30 to 40 minutes, or until the apples are tender and the juices bubble up through the top vents. (The length of baking time depends on the variety of apple.)

For an attractive glaze, 5 minutes before the pie is baked brush the pastry with 1 egg yolk mixed with 1 teaspoon milk.

Remove from the oven and set on a rack to cool. Serve warm, plain or with a wedge of sharp cheddar cheese or ice cream.

*Rhode Island Greenings, Baldwins, and Winesaps make delicious pies.

DUTCH APPLE PIE

Apple pie prepared in the Pennsylvania Dutch way has a topping of sweet crumbs instead of a crust.

FILLING	CRUMB TOPPING
6–7 cups (2 pounds) tart apples, sliced ⅓ inch thick	½ cup softened butter
⅔ cup sugar	½ cup brown sugar (packed)
1 teaspoon cinnamon	1 cup unsifted all-purpose flour
2 teaspoons lemon juice	Confectioners' sugar
⅛ teaspoon salt	
A 9-inch unbaked pastry shell	

To make the filling, combine the sliced apples with the sugar and cinnamon. Add the lemon juice and salt.

Turn the apples into the unbaked pastry shell.

For the topping, cream the butter and brown sugar together until soft and smooth. Add the flour and rub together with your fingertips until crumbs the size of small peas are formed. Sprinkle evenly over the apples. Chill for at least 15 minutes to set the crumbs.

Bake in a 425° oven for 30 to 40 minutes, or until the apples are tender and the crumbs are golden brown.

Cool on a rack and serve warm or at room temperature. Dust the top generously with confectioners' sugar before serving.

SOUR RED CHERRY PIE

A pie made from fresh sour cherries is a rare treat. Their season is limited, and they are usually available only where locally grown. Therefore, a version is given for frozen cherries. The use of canned cherries as a substitute is discouraged, as a pie made from them is not comparable.

4 cups sour red cherries (measured before pitting)	A 9-inch unbaked pastry shell with lattice top
1 cup sugar	¼ teaspoon almond extract
3 tablespoons flour	2 tablespoons butter
⅛ teaspoon salt	Vanilla ice cream (optional)

Stem and pit the cherries, saving the juices.

Combine the sugar, flour, and salt. Spread half the mixture in the unbaked pastry shell.

Combine the cherries and juice with the remaining flour mixture and let stand for 10 minutes or longer to draw more of the juices. Add the almond extract and mix well.

Pour into the pie shell and dot with the butter.

Moisten the pastry rim. Place strips of pastry over the top to form a lattice. Trim and flute the edge. (Before cutting, brush the strips with cream to form a shiny top, if desired.)

Bake on the lowest rack in a 450° oven for 15 minutes, then reduce the heat to 375° and bake 30 minutes longer. Cool on a rack.

Best served warm, with ice cream if desired.

Cherry Pie with Frozen Cherries: Combine a 16-ounce carton of frozen cherries (with sugar added) and 1½ tablespoons of flour, ⅓ cup of sugar, ⅛ teaspoon of salt, and 2 to 4 drops of almond extract. Pour into a 9-inch pastry shell. Dot with 2 tablespoons of butter. Cover with pastry or lattice. Bake at 400° for 35 minutes, or until the pastry is golden.

CHERRY PIE

Of course it is nicer when eating to have the cherries pitted, but either way is admissible. Put in the pie-plate plenty of fruit, sweeten well, and sprinkle with flour. No water is needed. The cherries will cook by the time the crust is done.

—Mrs. Owens' Cook Book and Useful Household Hints
by Frances E. Owens, 1888 Revised Edition (1884)

BLACKBERRY PIE

Berries release a great amount of juice during baking that seeps into the bottom crust. In this recipe the fruit and crust are cooked separately, eliminating the problem.

Pastry for a 9-inch double-crust pie	1 tablespoon minute tapioca
3½–4 cups blackberries	1 tablespoon butter (cut into small pieces)
¾ cup sugar	½–1½ teaspoons lemon juice
¼ teaspoon salt	Vanilla ice cream (optional)

Prepare the pastry. Divide the dough into two balls, making one a little larger than the other. Roll the larger ball to fit a 9-inch pie plate, then line the pan with the pastry. Flute the edges.

Roll the remaining dough as you would for a top crust. Sprinkle the top lightly with sugar and lightly roll in. Using an 8-inch pie plate rim as a guide, cut and trim away the excess pastry. Place on a cookie sheet.

Prick the pie shell and top crust well with a fork, then bake in a 400° oven for 10 to 12 minutes, or until golden brown. (After the first 5 minutes, check and prick any bubbles with a fork to release the air.) Cool on racks.

Rinse and pick over the blackberries, discarding the stems and soft berries. Combine the berries with the sugar, salt, tapioca, and butter in a saucepan. (Do not add the lemon juice.)

Cover and cook over low heat until the juices are thickened (about 10 minutes). Do not overcook or the berries will be mushy. Remove from the heat and cool slightly, then stir in the lemon juice to taste. (The amount will depend on the tartness of the berries.) Cool until just warm.

Fill the cooled pie shell with the warm filling. Set the sugared crust on top. Serve plain or with vanilla ice cream.

BLUEBERRY PIE

2½ cups (1 pint) blueberries
1 tablespoon flour
  Pastry for an 8-inch
  double-crust pie

½ cup sugar
⅛ teaspoon salt
1 teaspoon lemon juice
½ tablespoon butter

Rinse the berries, then remove the bits of stem and drain. Sift the flour over the berries and mix lightly to coat each one.

Line an 8-inch pie plate with pastry and trim it. Fill with the coated berries. Sprinkle with the sugar, salt, and lemon juice. Dot the top with the butter.

Moisten the rim of the pastry with cold water. Cover with the top crust and trim and flute the edges. Cut several slits in the top of the pastry to allow the steam to escape.

Bake on the lowest rack in a 400° oven for 30 to 35 minutes, or until the top crust is golden brown. Cool on a rack.

Serve slightly warm. If desired, top with plain or whipped heavy cream.

HUCKLEBERRY PIE

Carefully wash and drain the berries and sift flour over them until each berry becomes a little white ball. Allow a scanty cupful of sugar to each pie, stir it well into the fruit, and turn the latter into the pie plates. Cover each pie with an upper crust, and bake 1 hour; serve cold, with sugar sifted over the top. Flouring the berries in this way, while still a little wet from washing, will make just enough thickening to counteract the excessive amount of juice these berries are capable of giving off.

—Butterick's "Correct Cookery"
(1900)

STRAWBERRY AND RHUBARB PIE

Fresh rhubarb was often canned during season and stored, ready to be used for pies in midwinter. Since rhubarb readily takes to itself any flavor, whenever there was a scarcity of currants, gooseberries, apples, etc., the bulk of the pie was made with rhubarb, with a small portion of the other fruits added. Perhaps because of this basic quality, many old cookbooks referred to rhubarb as "pieplant."

1 cup small fresh strawberries (or large strawberries cut into halves or fourths)	1¼ cups sugar
	2 tablespoons flour
	A 9-inch unbaked pastry shell with lattice top
2 cups rhubarb (cut into ½-inch pieces)	1 tablespoon butter

Combine the strawberries with the rhubarb. Add the sugar and flour and mix well.

Pour into the pastry shell and dot the top with the butter. Arrange the pastry strips over the top in a lattice design. Flute the edge to form a high rim.

Bake on the lowest rack in a 425° oven for 10 minutes, then reduce the heat to 350° and bake 30 to 35 minutes longer.

Cool on a rack. Serve slightly warm.

DEEP-DISH RHUBARB PIE

Many cooks maintain that a proper rhubarb pie must contain eggs to modify the tart flavor. This one follows that advice and is baked without a bottom crust.

2 eggs	3 cups rhubarb (cut into ½-inch pieces)
1½ cups sugar	
3 tablespoons flour	Pastry for a 9-inch top
¼ teaspoon salt	Milk and sugar
1 teaspoon grated orange rind	Whipped cream (optional)

Beat the eggs until light. Gradually beat in the sugar, flour, salt, and orange rind. Fold in the rhubarb.

Pour into a buttered 9-inch pie plate. Cover with the pastry, trim the edge, and press with a fork to seal. Brush the top with milk and sprinkle it lightly with sugar. Cut several vents to allow the steam to escape.

Bake in a 350° oven for 40 to 45 minutes, or until the pastry is browned and the rhubarb is fork tender.

Serve slightly warm, plain or with whipped cream if desired.

PEACH CREAM PIE

6–7 (2 pounds) fresh peaches	1 cup sugar
A 9-inch unbaked pastry shell	⅛ teaspoon salt
	1 cup dairy sour cream
4 tablespoons plus 1 teaspoon flour	1 teaspoon vanilla

Scald the peaches in boiling water to cover for about 30 seconds to loosen the skins. Peel, pit, and slice thickly. (There should be 4 cups.) Arrange in the unbaked pastry shell, which has been rubbed with the teaspoon of flour.

Combine the 4 tablespoons of flour, the sugar, and the salt. Gradually stir in the sour cream, then the vanilla. Pour over the peaches, covering them completely and pushing any exposed peaches under.

Bake in a 400° oven for 45 to 50 minutes, or until the cream is set. Cool on a rack and serve slightly warm or at room temperature.

Note: If the peaches are very ripe, sweet, and juicy, reduce the cream and sugar to ¾ cup each.

FRUIT PIES IN VARIETY

In making pies from ripe summer fruit, raspberries, blackberries, damsons, cherries, &c., always take a deep plate, line it with paste, place in the middle an inverted teacup, and fill the plate with fruit. Brown sugar and spice to the taste. The cup thus placed, will receive the juice, which would otherwise escape at the edges of the pie. It will settle under the cup; which remove on cutting the pie.

—The Improved Housewife, or Book of Receipts
by Mrs. A. L. Webster, 1854 Edition (1843)

MOCK CHERRY PIE

These old-time pies combine split cranberries and raisins to simulate the taste of cherries.

1½ cups cranberries	3–4 drops almond extract
½ cup raisins	Pastry for an 8-inch
1 cup sugar	double-crust pie
1 tablespoon flour	1 teaspoon butter
2 tablespoons water	

Split the cranberries in half, one by one. Put into a colander and run cold water over them to remove as many seeds as possible.

Combine the cranberries with the raisins, sugar, flour, water, and almond extract.

Turn into the pastry-lined pie plate. Dot the top with the butter.

Moisten the rim of the pastry with cold water. Cover with the top crust, then trim and flute the edges. Cut several slits in the top of the pastry to allow the steam to escape.

Bake on the lowest rack in a 400° oven for 40 to 45 minutes, or until the pastry is browned and the juices bubble up through the center slits. Cool on a rack.

Serve slightly warm.

SOUR CREAM RAISIN PIE

Spicy and tangy.

2 eggs	1 cup dairy sour cream
1 cup sugar	2 tablespoons vinegar
½ teaspoon cinnamon	1 cup raisins
½ teaspoon cloves	An 8-inch unbaked pastry
¼ teaspoon salt	shell

Beat the eggs slightly. Combine the sugar, cinnamon, cloves, and salt. Add to the eggs and blend well.

Blend in the sour cream, vinegar, and raisins.

Pour into the unbaked pie shell. Bake at 425° for 10 minutes, then at 350° 25 to 30 minutes longer, or until the center is barely set.

Cool on a rack. Serve at room temperature.

FRESH PINEAPPLE PIE

Much better tasting than that made with canned pineapple.

2 eggs	2 cups coarsely chopped
1⅓ cups sugar	fresh pineapple
1 teaspoon flour	A 9-inch unbaked pastry
⅛ teaspoon salt	shell with lattice top
1 tablespoon lemon juice	1 tablespoon butter

Beat the eggs slightly. Stir in the sugar, flour, salt, and lemon juice. Add the pineapple and any juice; mix well.

Turn into the pastry-lined pie plate, dot with the butter, and cover with lattice strips, making a high fluted edge.

Bake at 450° for 10 minutes, then reduce the heat to 350° and bake 35 minutes longer, or until the filling bubbles up and the crust is brown.

Cool on a rack and serve warm.

Slicing pine-apples: The knife used for peeling a pine-apple should not be used for slicing it, as the rind contains an acid that is apt to cause a swollen mouth and sore lips. The Cubans use salt as an antidote for the ill effects of the peel.

—The White House Cook Book
by Mrs. F. L. Gillette and Hugo Ziemann, 1890 Edition (1887)

GREEN TOMATO PIE

Pumpkins, sweet potatoes, and green tomatoes all have been considered suitable vegetables for pie fillings since Colonial days. Unfortunately, the popularity of Green Tomato Pie seems to have slipped in recent years. The flavor is reminiscent of mincemeat.

4 tablespoons flour	½ teaspoon salt
½ cup plus 1 tablespoon sugar	½ teaspoon cinnamon
An 8-inch unbaked pastry	¼ teaspoon nutmeg
shell with lattice top	3 tablespoons vinegar
3 cups (1 pound) sliced green	2 tablespoons water
tomatoes	2 tablespoons butter

Sprinkle 2 tablespoons of flour and the tablespoon of sugar into the bottom of the pastry shell. Blend with the back of a spoon, spreading up the sides.

Core the tomatoes and trim any blemishes. Slice slightly less than ¼ inch thick. If the tomatoes are large, cut into halves or quarters, but leave the small tomatoes whole before slicing (the latter are best for this pie). Layer into the pastry shell.

Combine the ½ cup of sugar and the remaining 2 tablespoons of flour with the salt, cinnamon, and nutmeg. Gradually stir in the vinegar and water. Pour over the tomato slices and dot with the butter. Cover with lattice pastry.

Bake in a 400° oven for 40 to 45 minutes, or until the tomatoes test tender with a fork and the juices bubble up thick.

Cool on a rack. Serve slightly warm.

MARLBOROUGH PIE

In the early 1800s, pies that contained raw grated apples or stewed apples, cream, and eggs were called Marlborough Pies. Now they are also known as Apple Custard Pies.

3 eggs	Grated rind of ½ lemon
½ cup sweetened applesauce	2 tablespoons brandy
½ cup sugar	An 8-inch unbaked pastry
1 cup heavy cream	shell

Beat the eggs slightly. Stir in the applesauce, sugar, cream, and lemon rind. Mix well, then stir in the brandy.

Pour into the unbaked pastry shell, which has a high fluted edge, and bake at 425° for 10 minutes. Lower the heat to 350° and bake 30 to 35 minutes longer, or until a knife inserted halfway between the center and the pastry edge comes out clean, not milky-looking.

Place on a rack to cool. Serve slightly warm or at room temperature.

COCONUT CUSTARD PIE

Rich, satiny, smooth custard with coconut added.

4 eggs	2½ cups milk
A 9-inch unbaked pastry shell	½ teaspoon vanilla
½ cup sugar	½ teaspoon almond extract
¼ teaspoon salt	½ cup shredded coconut (preferably unsweetened)

Beat the eggs just enough to blend the yolks and whites thoroughly. If flaky pastry is used (see Standard Pastry for Single-Crust Pie, page 144), brush the bottom and sides of the pastry shell with about a teaspoon of the eggs and refrigerate for 30 minutes to help prevent a soggy crust.

Stir the sugar, salt, milk, vanilla, and almond extract into the eggs. Mix well, then strain.

Sprinkle the coconut over the bottom of the chilled pastry shell. Pour the custard mixture over the coconut. (To avoid any spills, add the last cup of filling to the shell after placing it on the oven rack.)

Bake in a 400° oven for 30 to 35 minutes, or until the filling is set, except for about an inch in the center. To test, shake the pan gently or insert a knife halfway between the outside and center of the custard (if the pie is done, the knife will come out clean, not milky-looking).

Remove from the oven and cool on a rack. Serve at room temperature.

Plain Custard Pie: Omit the coconut. Flavor with 1 teaspoon of vanilla and grate fresh nutmeg over the top of the pie as it comes from the oven. Bake for about 30 minutes.

CHESS PIE

Chess pies are said to have been based on an English recipe for Richmond Maids of Honor, whose basic ingredients were curds obtained from boiled milk, egg yolks, sugar, and lemon juice. The word "chess" is thought to have been a corruption of "cheese." As the recipe developed, the milk was omitted and replaced by butter. There are many versions; the one given is a Kentucky recipe said to be 125 years old.

3 eggs
2 tablespoons cornmeal
1 tablespoon flour
1/8 teaspoon salt*
1/4 teaspoon nutmeg
1 teaspoon vanilla

1 teaspoon vinegar
1/2 cup sweet butter (unsalted)
1 1/4 cups sugar
An 8-inch unbaked pastry shell

Beat the eggs slightly. Add the cornmeal, flour, salt, nutmeg, vanilla, and vinegar.

Melt the butter; add the sugar and stir until incorporated. Gradually beat into the egg mixture.

Pour into the unbaked pastry shell and bake at 350° for 30 to 35 minutes, or until the filling is set, begins to crack, and is golden brown. (It will rise as it bakes but settle as the pie cools.)

Cool until barely warm, or serve at room temperature.

*If salted butter is used, omit the salt.

PUMPKIN PIE

Pumpkin Pie was an early American invention, based on English Custard Pie. The Colonial women not only grew, cooked, and strained their favorite pie vegetable but often prepared the sauce in great quantities, added sugar and ginger, and stored it in a stone jar. It kept well for several months in cold weather and was on hand for future pie baking. When sugar was scarce, the pies were often partly sweetened with molasses.

*When peaches are in season,
it's time for this Fresh Peach Tart (page 184),
featuring honey-covered sliced peaches
decoratively arranged
over a tasty cream cheese filling.*

2 eggs
1 cup sugar
1½ cups strained cooked or
   canned pumpkin
½ teaspoon cinnamon
¼ teaspoon nutmeg

¼ teaspoon salt
¾ cup milk
¼ cup light cream
   A 9-inch unbaked pastry
   shell
   Whipped cream (optional)

Beat the eggs slightly. Blend in the sugar, pumpkin, cinnamon, nutmeg, and salt. Beat until thoroughly blended. Stir in the milk and cream.

Pour into the unbaked pie shell and bake at 425° for 15 minutes, then reduce the heat to 350° and bake 40 to 45 minutes longer, or until the blade of a knife inserted at the side of the filling comes out clean. (The soft center will set as the pie cools.)

Cool on a rack. Serve slightly warm or at room temperature, with or without lightly sweetened whipped cream.

Note: For a shiny top, blend the filling mixture long enough to dissolve the sugar, then let stand while preparing the crust. Mix again before filling the pastry shell.

PUMPKIN PIE

Bake as soon as the plates are filled, to prevent the crusts from becoming clammy.

—The Improved Housewife or Book of Receipts
by Mrs. A. L. Webster, 1854 Edition (1843)

COTTAGE CHEESE PIE

An old-time favorite.

2 cups cottage cheese	¼ teaspoon cinnamon
3 eggs	1 cup milk
1 cup sugar	A 9-inch unbaked pastry
2 tablespoons flour	shell

Press the cottage cheese through a coarse strainer. Set aside.

Beat the eggs slightly. Combine the sugar, flour, and cinnamon and stir into the eggs. Add the sieved cottage cheese and the milk; blend well.

Pour two-thirds of the mixture into the unbaked pastry shell. Set on a rack in the oven, then add the remainder (to prevent spilling).

Bake at 450° for 15 minutes, then reduce the heat to 325° and bake about 30 minutes longer, or until the center is almost set. (The filling will firm as it cools.)

Cool on a rack and serve at room temperature, or chilled if desired.

TRANSPARENT PIE

Rich with butter, this Southern favorite varies from state to state, from cook to cook. The one described here comes from Kentucky. In addition to the butter filling, the crust is dotted with jelly before baking. It is often called simply Jelly Pie.

1 cup sugar	An 8-inch unbaked pastry
4 tablespoons melted butter	shell
3 egg yolks	
1 tablespoon flour	MERINGUE
⅛ teaspoon salt	3 egg whites
½ cup water	⅛ teaspoon salt
1 teaspoon vanilla	1 teaspoon lemon juice
2 tablespoons tart jelly	6 tablespoons sugar

Combine the sugar, melted butter, and egg yolks. Beat until light and fluffy. Combine the flour, salt, water, and vanilla. Blend into the egg mixture.

Dot the unbaked pastry shell with the jelly, then pour in the filling. Bake at 350° for 30 to 35 minutes, removing from the oven just before the filling reaches the firm stage. Cool slightly while preparing the meringue.

Beat the egg whites with the salt until frothy. Add the lemon juice and beat until fluffy. Gradually beat in the sugar; continue beating until the meringue is glossy and the sugar is dissolved.

Spread on top of the pie, sealing the edges. Return to the 350° oven and bake 15 minutes longer, or until lightly browned.

BUTTERMILK PIE

Buttermilk pie is a member of the transparent pie family, which includes chess pie, the granddaddy of them all. As the pie bakes, the filling separates, forming a transparent layer at the bottom.

½ cup butter	1 cup buttermilk
2 cups sugar	1½ teaspoons vanilla
3 tablespoons flour	A 9-inch unbaked pastry
3 eggs	shell

Cream the butter with the sugar and flour until light. Beat in the eggs one at a time, then stir in the buttermilk and vanilla. Blend well. (The mixture will appear curdled.)

Pour into the unbaked pastry shell. Bake at 400° for 10 minutes, then reduce the heat to 325° and continue baking for 40 to 45 minutes, or until the filling is set and the top is golden brown. Test with a wooden pick in the center.

Cool on a rack. Serve at room temperature.

SHOOFLY PIE

The Pennsylvania Dutch bake several versions of a crumb pie flavored with molasses to which they give the name Shoofly Pie. Some are rather dry and are said to be good for "dunking." Others have a cakelike filling. Still others have a moist filling and are occasionally called Wet Bottom Shoofly, which is the type presented here.

FILLING
1 egg yolk
⅓ cup molasses
1½ teaspoons soda
⅔ cup boiling water

CRUMB MIXTURE
¾ cup sifted all-purpose flour

½ teaspoon cinnamon
½ teaspoon cloves
¼ teaspoon salt
½ cup light brown sugar
   (packed)
2 tablespoons soft butter
An 8-inch unbaked pastry
   shell

Beat the egg yolk slightly. Gradually blend in the molasses. Dissolve the soda in the boiling water, then stir into the molasses mixture. (It will foam up.) Set aside.

For the crumb mixture, sift the flour with the cinnamon, cloves, and salt. Combine with the brown sugar in a mixing bowl. Cut in the butter with a pastry blender until it looks like cornmeal.

Place half the crumbs in the bottom of the unbaked pastry shell. Spoon the molasses mixture carefully over the crumbs, then top with the remaining crumbs.

Bake at 450° for 10 minutes, then reduce the temperature to 350° and continue baking 15 minutes longer, or until the pie filling is set.

Cool on a rack to room temperature.

Molasses, if bought by the barrel or half-barrel, should be kept in the cellar. If bought in small quantities, it should be kept in a demijohn. No vessel should be corked or bunged, if filled with molasses, as it will swell and burst the vessel, or run over.

—Miss Beecher's Housekeeper and Healthkeeper
by Catharine E. Beecher (1873)

PECAN PIE

Until about fifty years ago, pecans were relatively unavailable to most cooks. Even in the localities where they grew wild, little effort was made to utilize them. Though the 1936 edition of Irma S. Rombauer's *The Joy of Cooking* included several recipes for cookies made with pecans, there was no recipe for pecan pie.

2 eggs	1 tablespoon melted butter
½ cup sugar	1¼ cups pecan halves
1 tablespoon flour	An 8-inch unbaked pastry
¼ teaspoon salt	shell
1 cup dark corn syrup	Whipped cream (optional)
1 teaspoon vanilla	

Beat the eggs with the sugar, flour, and salt. Add the corn syrup, vanilla, and melted butter and beat until well blended. Stir in the pecans.

Pour into the unbaked pastry shell and turn the rounded sides of the pecans up. Brush the edge of the pastry with cream.*

Bake at 300° for 60 minutes, or until the filling is set. (It should be a little less set in the center than around the edge; shake the pan slightly to test.)

Cool on a rack and serve at room temperature, with or without sweetened whipped cream.

Note: This pie can be baked a day in advance as the crust will not become soggy.

*At this low baking temperature, the crust will not brown without this addition.

OSGOOD PIE

Though the origin of this pie is unknown, recipes occasionally appear in regional cookbooks of Southern states where pecans are grown. The chewy filling, which includes raisins as well as nuts, has a thin, crisp meringue crust that develops while baking.

2 egg yolks	½ cup chopped pecans
1 cup sugar	½ cup chopped raisins
2 tablespoons melted butter	2 egg whites
½ teaspoon cinnamon	An 8-inch unbaked pastry
¼ teaspoon cloves	shell
2 teaspoons vinegar	

Beat the egg yolks slightly. Add the sugar, melted butter, cinnamon, cloves, and vinegar. Blend well. Add the pecans and raisins; mix well.

Beat the egg whites until stiff, then fold in.

Turn the filling into the pastry shell and spread evenly. Bake in a 350° oven for 30 to 35 minutes, or until set. (The egg whites will rise to the top, forming a thin crust. To test the filling, insert a wooden pick halfway between the outer crust and the center; it should come out clean. Also, when done the meringue will pull slightly away from the pastry.)

Cool on a rack and serve warm or at room temperature. Cut with a thin, sharp knife to avoid crumbling the meringue crust.

TWO-CRUST LEMON PIE

In presenting a similar recipe for Lemon Slice Pie, the authors of *Butterick's "Correct Cookery"* (1900) wrote: "There are, perhaps, more formulas for making pies of lemons than for any other way of using this delicious fruit, but this is the best of them all." The filling contains whole slices of unpeeled lemon.

FILLING	
1¼ cups sugar	4 tablespoons melted butter
2 tablespoons flour	½ cup water
⅛ teaspoon salt	1 large lemon
2 eggs	Pastry for an 8-inch
	double-crust pie

GLAZE	2 teaspoons sugar
Egg	¼ teaspoon cinnamon

To make the filling, combine the sugar, flour, and salt in a mixing bowl.

Beat the eggs until foamy, remove about 1 teaspoon for the glaze, and beat the remainder into the sugar mixture. Beat in the butter and water.

Cut the whole lemon into very thin slices. Discard the seeds and ends. (Do not peel.)

Pour half the filling into the unbaked pastry. Float the lemon slices on top, then cover with the remaining filling.

Moisten the edges of the pastry; cover with the pastry top. Trim and seal by pressing the tines of a fork around the edge.

For the glaze, brush the top with the reserved egg and sprinkle a mixture of the sugar and cinnamon over the top. Cut a few gashes to allow the steam to escape.

Bake at 375° for 30 to 35 minutes, or until the crust is golden brown. Cool on a rack and serve at room temperature.

In baking a pie that has two crusts, a strip of cotton cloth wrung from cold water and folded about the edge, resting on the upper crust and the under side of the tin rim, will prevent the juices from escaping during the cooking. This cloth should be pulled off as soon as the pie comes from the oven. Should the under crust come out of the oven wet and soggy, next time try a preventive of beaten egg. Beat both white and yolk together and with a soft brush paint the under crust. Place the pie tin in a cold place and when the egg has hardened pour in the filling and bake at once. When fruit fillings are used, the sugar should always be added after the fruit is in the pie tin, spreading it thickly on top of the fruit. To stir it through the fruit will cause it to candy on the under crust. Fruits generous in their own juices require the addition of little if any water.

—Butterick's "Correct Cookery"
(1900)

MONTGOMERY PIE

A Pennsylvania Dutch favorite, this pie is named for the county where it originated. It is known more familiarly as Lemon Cake Pie or Lemon Sponge Pie. As the filling bakes, a clear lemon layer forms on the bottom and a sponge rises to the top.

1 cup sugar	¼ cup lemon juice
3 tablespoons flour	Grated rind of 1 lemon
1 tablespoon butter	2 egg whites
2 egg yolks	An 8-inch unbaked pastry
1 cup milk	shell

Combine the sugar and flour in a mixing bowl. Add the butter and mix as for pie crust until crumbly.

Stir in the egg yolks, then the milk, lemon juice, and lemon rind.

Beat the egg whites until stiff but not dry. Blend into the lemon mixture.

To prevent spilling, pour three-fourths of the mixture into the unbaked pastry shell, set on a rack in the oven, then add the remainder. (The mixture is thin and the pie will be full, but the crust need not have a high fluted edge.)

Bake at 450° for 10 minutes, then reduce the heat to 350° and bake until set (about 20 to 25 minutes longer). The top should be golden brown and firm to the touch in the center.

Cool the pie on a rack to room temperature before cutting.

OLD-FASHIONED CREAM PIE

Cream pies have long been popular in the Midwest. The secret to the proper texture is knowing exactly when to remove the pie from the oven, so that it is neither too thick nor too runny.

2 tablespoons flour	An 8-inch unbaked pastry
1 tablespoon cornstarch	shell
¾ cup sugar	1 cup heavy cream
¼ teaspoon nutmeg	1 cup milk
2 tablespoons butter	

Mix the flour, cornstarch, sugar, nutmeg, and butter with a fork or a pastry blender until crumbly. Spread evenly in an unbaked pastry shell with a high fluted edge. Pour in the cream and the milk (use just enough to almost fill the shell).

Bake in a 425° oven until the pastry is lightly browned and a crust has formed on the filling (about 10 minutes).

Break the filling crust gently with a rubber spatula, being careful not to puncture the pastry underneath. Stir the mixture carefully.

Reduce the temperature to 350° and bake until the filling bubbles up thick and a light brown crust has formed on the top (about 45 minutes longer).

Set on a rack to cool slightly. Serve warm.

TEXAS CREAM PIE

Line a pie-plate with pie-paste. Then put
A layer of butter.
A layer of sugar.
A layer of flour.
A layer of sugar.
Pour milk over and bake.

—Mrs. Owens' Cook Book and Useful Household Hints
by Frances E. Owens, 1888 Revised Edition (1884)

Note: The recipe was credited to Mrs. A. G. Leffet, Dallas, Texas.

COCONUT MACAROON PIE

Somewhat chewy, like macaroons.

½ cup soft butter
1½ cups sugar
¼ teaspoon salt
¼ cup flour
2 eggs

½ cup milk
½ teaspoon vanilla
1½ cups shredded coconut
A 9-inch unbaked pastry
shell

Beat the butter until creamy. Gradually beat in the sugar, salt, and flour. Add the eggs one at a time, beating well after each addition.

Stir in the milk and vanilla. Fold in 1 cup of the shredded coconut.

Pour the mixture into the pastry shell and sprinkle the remaining ½ cup of coconut over the top.

Bake in a 325° oven for 60 minutes, or until the coconut is golden and the filling is firm.

Cool on a rack and serve at room temperature.

PASTE FOR PUDDINGS AND ICES

This is an article which, if the laws of health were obeyed, would be banished from every table; for it unites the three evils—animal fat, cooked animal fat, and heavy bread. Nothing in the whole range of cooking is more indigestible than rich pie-crust, especially when, as bottom crust, it is made still worse by being soaked, or slack-baked. Still, as this work does not profess to leave out unwholesome dishes, but only to set forth an abundance of healthful ones, and the reasons for preferring them, the best directions will be given for making the best kind of paste.

—Miss Beecher's Housekeeper and Healthkeeper
by Catharine E. Beecher (1873)

BUTTERSCOTCH PIE

An old-timer with real butterscotch flavor. The secret is in the precooking of the brown sugar and butter with part of the milk before combining it with the remaining filling ingredients.

FILLING
3 tablespoons butter
2 cups brown sugar (packed)
2 cups milk
4 tablespoons flour
½ teaspoon salt
3 egg yolks
1 teaspoon vanilla

An 8-inch baked pastry shell

MERINGUE
3 egg whites
¼ teaspoon cream of tartar
6 tablespoons sugar
½ teaspoon vanilla

To make the filling, melt the butter in a heavy saucepan. Stir in the brown sugar and ½ cup of milk. Cook, stirring until the sugar is dissolved and the mixture comes to a boil, then cook over low heat for 5 minutes without stirring. Remove from the heat.

Combine the flour and salt. Beat the egg yolks slightly. Blend in the remaining 1½ cups of milk, then gradually stir into the flour mixture.

Slowly stir the egg yolk mixture into the hot caramel sauce. Cook, stirring until the mixture comes to a boil and thickens. Continue cooking and stirring over low heat 3 or 4 minutes longer to take away the flour taste.

Remove from the heat, let cool for a few minutes, then stir in the vanilla. Cover and cool to lukewarm. Turn into the cooled, baked pastry shell.

To make the meringue, beat the egg whites with the cream of tartar until soft peaks form. Gradually beat in the sugar. Continue beating until stiff and glossy, then beat in the vanilla.

Pile the meringue lightly over the filling, sealing to the edges. Bake in a 325° oven until lightly browned (about 15 minutes).

Cool to room temperature, away from drafts, before serving.

LEMON PIE

Juice and grated rind of 1 lemon.
1 cup sugar.
1 cup water.
1 tablespoon corn starch or 2 of flour.
2 yolks of eggs well beaten.

Mix all together and cook in a basin over water. Line a pie-plate with paste, put in the mixture and bake till the crust is done. Then whip the whites of eggs to a stiff froth with 2 tablespoons of sugar, spread over and brown in the oven.

—Mrs. Owens' Cook Book and Useful Household Hints
by Frances E. Owens, 1888 Revised Edition (1884)

LEMON MERINGUE PIE

In the 1800s meringues for pies were not as high nor as tender as those of today. They required only one tablespoon of sugar (often powdered) for each egg white, whereas at least two are recommended today.

FILLING	Grated rind of ½ lemon
1½ cups sugar	A 9-inch baked pastry shell
7 tablespoons cornstarch	
¼ teaspoon salt	MERINGUE
1½ cups hot water	3 egg whites
3 egg yolks	⅛ teaspoon salt
2 tablespoons butter	2 teaspoons lemon juice
½ cup fresh lemon juice	7 tablespoons sugar

To make the filling, combine the sugar, cornstarch, and salt in a heavy saucepan. Gradually blend in the hot water. Bring to a boil over medium heat, stirring constantly. Boil, stirring 1 minute longer, or until the bubbles actually break on top.

Beat the egg yolks slightly. Gradually stir in part of the cornstarch mixture, then return to the remainder. Return to a boil, then boil, stirring 1 minute longer.

Remove from the heat and blend in the butter, then slowly stir in the lemon juice and rind.

Cover and cool without stirring until lukewarm, then turn into the cooled pastry shell.

To make the meringue, beat the egg whites with the salt and lemon juice until soft peaks form, then gradually beat in the sugar. Continue beating until the meringue is stiff and glossy and the sugar is dissolved.

Pile the meringue onto the pie filling, starting at the edges and attaching securely to prevent shrinking, then working toward the center. Swirl with the back of a spoon to form an attractive top. Bake in a 400° oven for 8 to 10 minutes, or until delicately brown.

Cool at room temperature, away from drafts.

VINEGAR PIE

This tangy old-fashioned pie is similar to Lemon Meringue Pie and surely must be its predecessor. The filling is amber in color.

FILLING
1 cup sugar
3 tablespoons flour
1/3 cup cider vinegar
2 egg yolks
1 cup water
1 tablespoon butter
  An 8-inch baked pastry
  shell

MERINGUE
2 egg whites
1/8 teaspoon salt
1 teaspoon vinegar
4 tablespoons sugar

To make the filling, combine the sugar and flour in the top of a double boiler. Stir in the cider vinegar, then the egg yolks and water.

Cook over simmering water, stirring constantly, until smooth and very thick (about 20 minutes).

Remove from the heat and add the butter, blending it in well. Cover the pan to prevent a skin from forming and cool to lukewarm, then spoon the filling into the cooled, baked pastry shell.

To make the meringue, beat the egg whites with the salt until frothy. Then add the vinegar and gradually add the sugar. Continue beating until the meringue is stiff and glossy and the sugar is completely dissolved.

Pile the meringue onto the pie filling, sealing to the edges to prevent shrinking and weeping.

Bake in a 350° oven for 10 to 15 minutes, or until delicately browned. Cool gradually. Serve at room temperature.

LEMON CREAM PIE

A cream pie delicately flavored with lemon juice and grated lemon rind.

FILLING
1¼ cups sugar
5 tablespoons flour
4 tablespoons cornstarch
⅛ teaspoon salt
2 cups milk
3 egg yolks
7 teaspoons lemon juice
Grated rind of 1 lemon

3 tablespoons butter
A 9-inch baked pastry shell

MERINGUE
3 egg whites
¼ teaspoon cream of tartar
1 teaspoon lemon juice
6 tablespoons sugar

To make the filling, combine the sugar, flour, cornstarch, and salt in a heavy saucepan. Gradually stir in the milk. Bring to a full boil, stirring constantly, then boil, stirring 1 minute longer.

Remove from the heat and stir about half the mixture into the slightly beaten egg yolks, then blend into the hot mixture in the saucepan. Return to a boil and boil for 2 or 3 minutes, stirring constantly.

Remove from the heat. Blend in the lemon juice, lemon rind, and butter. Cover to prevent a skin from forming and cool to lukewarm. Turn the filling into the cooled, baked pastry shell.

To make the meringue, beat the egg whites with the cream of tartar and lemon juice until the mixture mounds softly. Gradually beat in the sugar. Continue beating until the meringue is stiff and glossy and the sugar is completely dissolved.

Pile onto the pie filling, sealing the edges to prevent shrinking. Swirl or pull up points for a decorative top.

Bake at 400° for 8 to 10 minutes, or until delicately browned. Cool away from drafts at room temperature for at least 2 hours.

BANANA CREAM PIE

The filling for this modern cream pie is cooked on top of the stove, cooled, poured over sliced bananas in a baked pie shell, and topped with whipped cream.

FILLING

⅔ cup sugar
3 tablespoons cornstarch
¼ teaspoon salt
3 cups milk
3 egg yolks
2 tablespoons butter
1 teaspoon vanilla

A 9-inch baked pastry shell
3 large bananas

TOPPING

1 cup heavy cream
1 tablespoon sugar
½ teaspoon vanilla

For the filling, blend the sugar, cornstarch, and salt in a heavy saucepan. Heat the milk until bubbles appear around the edge. Gradually blend into the cornstarch mixture. Cook over medium heat, stirring constantly until the mixture boils and thickens, then boil for 1 minute.

Beat the egg yolks slightly. Gradually stir in about one-third of the milk mixture, then return to the remainder in the saucepan. Boil, stirring 1 minute longer.

Remove from the heat and blend in the butter. Let cool slightly and stir in the vanilla. Cover and cool to room temperature, stirring occasionally.

Pour a little of the cooled filling over the bottom of the cooled pastry shell. Slice the bananas directly over the filling, spreading evenly. To prevent them from browning, cover them immediately with the remaining filling.

For the topping, whip the cream until slightly thickened, then beat in the sugar and vanilla. Continue beating until almost stiff. Spread over the filling. Refrigerate until served.

Pastry cannot be easily excluded from the menu of the New Englander. Who can dream of a Thanksgiving dinner without a pie! The last decade has done much to remove pies from the daily bill of fare, and in their place are found delicate puddings and seasonable fruits.

—The Boston Cooking-School Cook Book
by Fannie Merritt Farmer, 1920 Edition (1896)

GRAHAM CRACKER PIE

A cream filling in a crumb crust, topped with meringue and more crumbs.

CRUMB CRUST
½ cup butter
1½ cups graham cracker
　crumbs
¼ cup sugar

CREAM FILLING
½ cup sugar
¼ teaspoon salt
1 tablespoon cornstarch
1 tablespoon flour
2 cups milk

2 egg yolks
2 teaspoons butter
1 teaspoon vanilla

MERINGUE
2 egg whites
½ teaspoon salt
¼ teaspoon cream of tartar
½ teaspoon vanilla
4 tablespoons confectioners'
　sugar

For the crust, melt the butter in a skillet. Remove from the heat and add the graham cracker crumbs and sugar; mix well. Reserve a scant ½ cup for the top of the pie. Press the remainder into a well-greased 9-inch pie plate.

For the filling, combine the sugar, salt, cornstarch, and flour in the top of a double boiler. Gradually stir in the milk. Set over simmering water and cook, stirring constantly until thickened (about 10 minutes).

Beat the egg yolks slightly and gradually beat in about half of the hot mixture. Add to the remaining mixture in the double boiler and cook 3 or 4 minutes longer, or until the filling barely holds its shape when the spoon is drawn through it. Remove from the heat; blend in the butter, then the vanilla. Pou into the crumb crust and allow to cool slightly.

To make the meringue, beat the egg whites with the salt, cream of tartar, and vanilla until the mixture mounds softly. Gradually beat in the sugar and continue beating until stiff.

Spread the meringue over the pie filling, covering the edges of the crust. Sprinkle the reserved crumbs over the top.

Bake in a 350° oven for 20 to 25 minutes, or until the crumbs are crisp and the meringue feels firm. Cool away from drafts. Serve at room temperature.

CHOCOLATE FUDGE PIE

Dark and rich, like fudge in a pastry shell, topped with whipped cream.

FILLING
⅞ cup sugar (1 cup less 2 tablespoons)
2 tablespoons flour
½ teaspoon salt
¼ cup heavy cream
2 egg yolks
1 cup boiling water
1½-ounce squares unsweetened chocolate
4 tablespoons butter
1 teaspoon vanilla

An 8-inch baked pastry shell

WHIPPED CREAM TOPPING
¾ cup heavy cream
1 tablespoon confectioners' sugar
¼ teaspoon vanilla
½-ounce square unsweetened chocolate

For the filling, combine the sugar, flour, and salt in a heavy saucepan. Stir in the cream and egg yolks. Gradually stir in the boiling water. Cook over low heat, stirring constantly until the mixture thickens and comes to a full boil. Boil for 1 minute.

Remove from the heat and add the unmelted chocolate and the butter. Stir until the chocolate and butter are melted. Blend in the vanilla.

Set the saucepan in a bowl of cold water. Beat the filling until it is lukewarm, thick, and glossy like fudge. Turn into the cooled, baked pastry shell. Chill thoroughly.

For the topping, whip the cream until almost stiff, then beat in the confectioners' sugar and vanilla. Spread over the top of the chilled filling. Grate the chocolate over the top with a vegetable peeler.

Return to the refrigerator, but remove at least 20 minutes before serving.

EGGNOG CHIFFON PIE

Chiffon pies were invented in 1921 by a professional baker who lived in Iowa. By beating egg whites with a fruit-flavored syrup until the mixture was light and fluffy, he achieved a filling that his mother said looked like a pile of chiffon. This same baker also invented the crumb crust, supposedly for his "pile of chiffon."

1 envelope unflavored gelatin	¼ cup light rum
¼ cup cold water	½ teaspoon lemon juice
3 egg yolks	½ cup heavy cream
1 cup sugar	3 egg whites
¼ teaspoon nutmeg (scant)	A 9-inch baked pastry shell
¼ teaspoon salt	with high fluted rim
1 cup light cream	Freshly grated nutmeg

Sprinkle the gelatin over the cold water; set aside to soften.

Beat the egg yolks with ½ cup of sugar, the nutmeg, and the salt. Heat the light cream until bubbles appear around the edge, then gradually stir into the egg yolk mixture. Cook over hot, not boiling, water, stirring until the mixture thickens slightly and will coat a metal spoon. Remove from the heat.

Add the gelatin to the hot custard mixture, stirring until the gelatin is dissolved. Chill, stirring occasionally until the mixture begins to set. Add the rum and lemon juice and beat just until smooth.

Whip the heavy cream until it mounds softly but is not stiff. Fold into the gelatin mixture.

Beat the egg whites until soft peaks form, then gradually beat in the remaining ½ cup of sugar until the mixture is stiff and glossy. Fold into the gelatin mixture.

Pour into the cooled pastry shell. Sprinkle with freshly grated nutmeg and chill until firm. Remove from the refrigerator 20 minutes before serving.

BLACK BOTTOM PIE

Recipes for Black Bottom Pie began to appear in cookbooks around the turn of the twentieth century, when gelatin was still sold in isinglass sheets as well as in the newer granulated form. Part of the filling is colored with chocolate and spread over a crumb shell before adding the remaining filling—thus the unusual name. This version has chunks of chocolate spread over the crust, an idea from a Columbus, Ohio, hotel that featured the pie during the 1950s.

GRAHAM CRACKER CRUST
- 4 tablespoons butter
- 1⅓ cups graham cracker crumbs
- 1 4-ounce bar Germans' sweet chocolate

FILLING
- 1 envelope unflavored gelatin
- ¼ cup cold water
- 3 egg yolks
- ½ cup sugar
- ¾ cup milk
- 3 tablespoons brandy
- 3 egg whites

TOPPING
- 1 cup heavy cream
- 2 tablespoons sugar
- 1 tablespoon brandy

To make the crust, melt the butter, add the graham cracker crumbs, and stir until all the crumbs are moistened. Press evenly and firmly over the bottom and sides of a 9-inch pie plate. Cut the chocolate into small chunks and distribute evenly over the bottom.

For the filling, sprinkle the gelatin over the water and set aside to soften.

Beat the egg yolks slightly in the top of a double boiler. Stir in ¼ cup of sugar, then the milk. Set over simmering water and cook, stirring until the mixture is thickened and coats a spoon. (Do not boil.) Remove from the heat, add the gelatin, and stir until dissolved.

Chill the custard, stirring occasionally until the mixture mounds when dropped from a spoon. Add the brandy and beat just until smooth.

Beat the egg whites until soft peaks form. Then gradually beat in the remaining ¼ cup of sugar. Continue beating until stiff and glossy. Fold into the gelatin mixture.

Pour into the graham cracker crust and chill until firm.

For the topping, whip the cream until it thickens, then gradually beat in the sugar and the brandy. Spread over the chilled filling.

Return the pie to the refrigerator, but remove 20 minutes before serving. It should be served cold, but not icy cold.

NESSELRODE PIE

Nesselrode is the name of a classic frozen pudding containing chestnut puree, raisins, and candied fruits. It is flavored with maraschino liquor. The dessert was created by a French chef in the nineteenth century and named for his master, a Russian count. In its American adaptation, Nesselrode is the culinary name for a rum- or brandy-flavored chiffon pie filling that contains candied fruits.

1 envelope unflavored gelatin	½ cup heavy cream
½ cup sugar	2 tablespoons chopped
¼ teaspoon salt	blanched almonds
1½ cups light cream	4–6 tablespoons diced mixed
2 egg yolks	candied fruit
¼ cup light rum	A 9-inch baked pastry shell
2 egg whites	

Combine the gelatin with ¼ cup of sugar and the salt in the top of a double boiler. Gradually stir in the light cream. Cook over hot water, stirring until the gelatin has dissolved.

Beat the egg yolks slightly, then gradually stir in the gelatin mixture. Return the mixture to the double boiler. Cook, stirring constantly until it thickens slightly and will coat a metal spoon. Remove from the heat, pour into a bowl, and chill, stirring occasionally until the mixture mounds slightly when dropped from a spoon. Beat in the rum just until smooth.

Beat the egg whites until soft peaks form, then gradually beat in the remaining ¼ cup of sugar. Continue beating until stiff and glossy. Fold into the gelatin mixture.

Whip the cream until it mounds softly. Fold it into the gelatin mixture, then fold in the almonds and mixed candied fruit.

Turn into the cooled pastry shell and chill until set. Remove from the refrigerator 20 minutes before serving.

GLAZED STRAWBERRY PIE

Although this pie is probably derived from French tarts, the American version with strawberries became well-known shortly after the fast-food chains became popular in the 1950s. Many of the franchise houses in the Midwest featured this pie.

1 quart fresh strawberries
A 9-inch baked pastry shell
1 cup sugar
1 cup plus 3 tablespoons
   water
3 tablespoons cornstarch

⅛ teaspoon salt
1 teaspoon lemon juice
2 teaspoons butter
   Red food coloring
1 cup heavy cream

Rinse, drain, and remove the hulls from the strawberries. Crush enough of the softest, least attractive ones to fill 1 cup. Arrange the remaining berries, points up, in the cooled pastry shell.

Pour the crushed berries into a saucepan. Stir in the sugar and the cup of water. Bring to a boil, stirring until the sugar is dissolved. Remove from the heat, then strain into another saucepan.

Blend the cornstarch, salt, and remaining 3 tablespoons of water. Stir into the berry syrup. Cook, stirring constantly until thickened. Remove from the heat and stir in the lemon juice and butter. Add a few drops of red food coloring to make an attractive bright color. Cool for 1 minute.

Pour the warm syrup over the berries, making certain that all the berries are covered.

Chill thoroughly (at least 2 hours). When ready to serve, whip the cream until fluffy and spoon around the edge, leaving the center open; or pass the whipped cream separately.

BERRY TARTS

Line small pie-tins with pie-crust, and bake. Just before ready to use, fill the tarts with strawberries, blackberries, raspberries, or whatever berries are in season. Sprinkle over each tart a little sugar; after adding berries add also to each tart a tablespoonful of sweet cream. They form a delicious addition to the breakfast table.

—The White House Cook Book
by Mrs. F. L. Gillette and Hugo Ziemann, 1890 Edition (1887)

LIME CHIFFON PIE

This pie is lightly flavored with lime juice. It is golden yellow, flecked with line rind.

FILLING
1½ teaspoons unflavored gelatin
3 tablespoons cold water
4 egg yolks
¾ cup sugar
3 tablespoons fresh lime juice (1½ limes)
Grated rind of 1 lime

4 egg whites
A 9-inch baked graham cracker crust (page 147)

WHIPPED CREAM TOPPING
1 cup heavy cream
1 tablespoon confectioners' sugar

To make the filling, sprinkle the gelatin over the cold water. Set aside to soften.

Beat the egg yolks with ½ cup of sugar in a saucepan until light. Stir in the lime juice and rind and softened gelatin.

Cook over low heat, stirring constantly until the sugar and gelatin are dissolved and the mixture is creamy. (Do not boil.)

Chill, stirring occasionally until the mixture mounds lightly when dropped from a spoon.

Beat the egg whites until soft peaks form; then gradually beat in the remaining ¼ cup of sugar. Continue beating until stiff and glossy. Stir one-third of the egg whites into the gelatin mixture to lighten it, then fold in the remainder until blended evenly.

Pile into the cooled, baked crust and chill.

Just before serving, make the topping by whipping the cream with the confectioners' sugar until almost stiff. Spread over the chilled filling. Serve cold.

KEY LIME PIE

Wild limes, known as Key limes, which are smaller and more astringent than ordinary limes, are grown in Key West, Florida. After sweetened condensed milk was manufactured in 1858, a thrifty conch settler in Key West was inspired to combine these two ingredients to create Key Lime Pie.

FILLING
4 egg yolks
1 egg white
1 14-ounce can sweetened
    condensed milk
½ cup fresh lime juice*
¼ teaspoon salt

A 9-inch baked pastry shell

MERINGUE
3 egg whites
½ teaspoon cream of tartar
6 tablespoons sugar

To make the filling, beat the egg yolks and the egg white until they are thick and lemon-colored and fall back, making a ribbon, when the beaters are raised. Add the sweetened condensed milk, lime juice, and salt. Stir until well blended (do not beat).

Pour the filling into the baked pastry shell.

To make the meringue, beat the egg whites with the cream of tartar until they form rounded peaks, then gradually beat in the sugar. Continue beating until the meringue is stiff and glossy and the sugar has completely dissolved. Spread over the filling, sealing the edges well to prevent shrinking. Swirl it decoratively with the back of a spoon.

Bake in a 425° oven 5 to 7 minutes, or until delicately browned. Cool away from drafts, then refrigerate until time to serve.

Note: The filling for this pie is not cooked.

*Key limes are rarely found outside Florida. The amount of juice given here is based on the acidity of the more readily available and common Persian lime. The flavor of the filling is mellow, not tart.

FRENCH SILK PIE

This pie is very different from other chocolate pies. The filling is an uncooked blend of butter, chocolate, sugar, and eggs. When prepared properly, it is as smooth as silk. To make this filling, an electric mixer is almost a necessity.

1 1-ounce square unsweetened chocolate	2 eggs An 8-inch baked pastry
½ cup butter	shell or graham cracker
¾ cup sugar	crust
1 teaspoon vanilla	½ cup heavy cream

Melt the chocolate over hot water. Set aside to cool slightly.

Cream the butter with an electric mixer until fluffy. Gradually beat in the sugar and continue beating until creamy. Beat in the cooled chocolate and the vanilla.

Add the eggs one at a time, beating for 3 minutes after the first addition and 5 minutes after the second, or until the mixture is smooth and the sugar is completely dissolved.

Pour into the baked and cooled pastry shell or crumb crust. Refrigerate for several hours until firm. (The pastry crust will remain crisp for at least 12 hours.)

When ready to serve, whip the cream and spread it over the pie. Shave additional unsweetened chocolate over the top if desired.

FRESH PEACH TART

1 cup all-purpose flour	3-4 ripe medium peaches,
¼ cup sugar	peeled and cut into ½-inch
1 teaspoon grated lemon rind	wedges
⅓ cup butter or margarine	1 8-ounce package cream
1 egg yolk	cheese, softened
2 tablespoons honey	3 tablespoons light cream
2 tablespoons lemon juice	

Mix the flour, sugar, and grated lemon rind in a bowl. Cut in the butter or margarine until the particles are the size of peas. Add the egg yolk and stir with a fork to mix. Gather into a ball and press evenly with lightly floured fingertips into a fluted 9-inch loose-bottomed tart pan, covering the bottom and sides completely. Bake in a 375° oven for 15 minutes, or until golden brown. Cool on a cake rack.

Drizzle the honey and 1 tablespoon of lemon juice over the peaches, toss gently, cover, and let stand for 10 minutes.

Mix the cream cheese and cream, add the remaining lemon juice, and beat until smooth and blended. Remove the rim from the tart pan and spread the bottom of the tart with the cream cheese mixture.

Arrange the peach wedges in overlapping rows on the mixture and pour peach juice on top. Serve at once in wedges. Serves 8.

LEMON ANGEL PIE

Angel Pie is an American variation of the German Schaum Torte, which consists of two crisp layers of meringue with filling between the layers. The American version is a single layer of meringue baked in a pie plate, filled, and refrigerated until soft and tender. Lemon filling is the most popular.

4 egg yolks	Grated rind of 1 lemon
⅔ cup plus 2 tablespoons sugar	1 cup heavy cream
⅓ cup lemon juice	Meringue Crust for Angel Pie (page 148)

Beat the egg yolks in the top of a double boiler until thick and lemon-colored. Gradually beat in the ⅔ cup of sugar, then the lemon juice and rind. Cook over hot water, stirring constantly until very thick (about 8 to 10 minutes). Cool, stirring occasionally.

Whip the cream until it begins to thicken, then gradually beat in the 2 tablespoons of sugar and continue beating until stiff.

Spread a thin layer of the whipped cream over the bottom and sides of the meringue crust (to prevent the acid in the filling from causing the meringue to disintegrate). Cover with the lemon filling and top with the remaining whipped cream.

Chill for 12 to 24 hours before serving to allow the meringue to soften.

MOCHA ANGEL PIE

4 1-ounce squares
   semisweet chocolate
¼ cup cold, strong black
   coffee

1 teaspoon vanilla
1 cup heavy cream
   Pecan Meringue Crust for
   Angel Pie (page 148)

Melt the chocolate in the coffee in a heavy saucepan over low heat, stirring until well blended. Cool, then stir in the vanilla.

Whip the cream until stiff. Fold into the chocolate mixture.

Spoon into the meringue crust. Refrigerate for 12 hours or overnight before serving.

RASPBERRY CREAM ANGEL PIE

⅔ cup sugar
⅓ cup sifted all-purpose flour
¼ teaspoon salt
2 cups milk
4 egg yolks

1 tablespoon butter
1½ teaspoons vanilla
   Meringue Crust for Angel
   Pie (page 148)
1 cup fresh red raspberries

Combine the sugar, flour, and salt in the top of a double boiler. Gradually stir in the milk. Set over simmering water and cook, stirring constantly until thickened (about 10 minutes).

Beat the egg yolks slightly and gradually stir in part of the milk mixture. Return to the double boiler and cook, stirring 3 or 4 minutes longer, or until the mixture barely holds its shape when the spoon is drawn through it.

Remove from the heat and blend in the butter, then the vanilla. Cool, stirring occasionally to prevent a skin from forming.

Spoon the cooled filling into the meringue crust. Place a piece of plastic wrap directly on the filling to prevent a skin. Chill for at least 12 hours, or overnight if desired.

When ready to serve, remove the plastic carefully and arrange the raspberries over the top of the filling.

V

Simple
Fruit Desserts

WHEN THE first settlers arrived in America, they found a variety of familiar fruits and berries growing wild. Blackberries, raspberries, gooseberries, and currants were plentiful on both sides of the Atlantic. Huckleberries and blueberries were similar to the English bilberries; strawberries, though larger than the European dwarf variety, were already favorites. New to them were the cranberries they found growing in bogs. They called them craneberries because the blossom resembled the head and neck of the crane.

There were wild beach plums, persimmons, and several varieties of cherries, both sweet and sour. But there was only one variety of apple—the crab apple. So they had to import this favorite fruit from England until the slips they had planted were strong enough to bear fruit.

Although many of these fruits and berries might have been eaten raw, they were usually preserved or dried; converted into jellies, ciders, and wines; or used in pies or baked or boiled puddings.

During the Colonial period these wild fruits were cultivated, and eventually peaches, pears, oranges, and melons became available. Exotic fruits such as bananas, coconuts, and pineapples were imported.

Perhaps because of a preference for sweet desserts adopted from English ancestry, Americans have seldom eaten raw fruits as dessert. Hence, there are few simple desserts made with fresh fruits that can be considered as old-fashioned. Among those that are, many are of English origin, such as Flummery, Summer Pudding, or even Baked Apples.

American recipes in this category are mostly Southern favorites, such as Ambrosia, Fried Peaches, and Fried Bananas. The fresh fruit desserts the whole country has endorsed are those made from strawberries, the luscious, large berries that are descendants of the strawberries the early settlers found growing in the 1600s.

Preparing Fresh Fruits

1. Select fruits that are fully ripe but still firm.

2. Berries, cranberries, and cherries should be picked over. Bits of stems and bruised fruit should be discarded. Rinse the fruit quickly in cold water and dry on paper toweling. Remove any seeds, and the hulls from strawberries, after rinsing.

3. Peaches, pears, and apples should be brushed with lemon juice or dropped into cold, salted water (1 teaspoon to 1 quart) after peeling and cutting to prevent darkening. Leave in only a few minutes.

4. Apples should be cored with an apple corer for neatness. Pears, unless left whole and cored, should have the cores removed with a melon ball cutter or a measuring teaspoon—again only for neatness.

5. To peel peaches easily, place them in boiling water to cover for about 30 seconds (or longer) to loosen the skins, then cool them in cold water. The skins should slip off easily.

Note: The recipes included here are those that are simple to prepare and therefore retain the basic qualities of the individual fruits. See the Index for other recipes using fruits.

GLAZED APPLES

These whole peeled apples are simmered in syrup to produce a glaze that bubbles into a foamy crust.

4 tart, medium-size apples*	**½ cup water**
1 cup sugar	**Light or heavy cream**

Peel the apples and core them with an apple corer. Place them in a saucepan just large enough so that each apple is resting on the bottom.

Combine the sugar and water; pour into the saucepan at the sides. Bring to a boil over medium-high heat. Boil until the apples are cooked through and the syrup foams and settles on the tops of the apples in a foamy glaze when the pan is removed from the heat.

Remove the apples from the syrup to dessert dishes and cool. Serve chilled or at room temperature, with the cream poured around the apples (not over the top).

*Cortland, Rome Beauty, and McIntosh hold their shape well. Cortland does not turn brown when exposed to air.

HOT BAKED APPLES

Filled with raisins and baked and basted until glazed.

½ cup raisins	**6 tablespoons butter**
1 cup sugar	**3 tablespoons brown sugar**
1 cup water	**Heavy cream**
6 large baking apples*	

Soak the raisins in hot water to cover for 5 minutes, then drain.

Combine the sugar and water in a saucepan. Bring to a boil, then simmer for 2 minutes. Remove from the heat.

Wash the apples and core them with an apple corer. Pare them about one-third of the way down from the stem end.

*Cortland, and McIntosh (which cook faster), are varieties that hold their shape and have deep red skins.

Place the apples in a shallow 12x8-inch baking dish, pared ends upright. Fill the cavities with the raisins and add 1 tablespoon of the butter to each. Pour the hot syrup over the tops.

Bake in the middle of a 375° oven for 20 to 30 minutes, or until the apples are almost tender, basting occasionally with the syrup. Remove from the oven and turn the heat to 500°.

Place a little of the brown sugar in each of the cavities and sprinkle the remaining sugar over the pared surfaces.

Return the apples to the oven. Bake until the sugar in the cavities has melted and the sugar on the peeled sections is lightly browned. Baste once or twice to give the apples a varnished appearance.

Transfer the apples to individual dessert bowls. Serve hot with the syrup and with heavy cream poured into the sides of the bowls. Serves 6.

BAKED APPLES

Get nice fruit, a little tart and juicy, but not sour; clean them nicely, and bake in a moderate oven—regulated so as to have them done in about an hour; when the skin cracks and the pulp breaks through in every direction they are done and ready to take out. Serve with white sugar sprinkled over them.

—The White House Cook Book
by Mrs. F. L. Gillette and Hugo Ziemann, 1890 Edition (1887)

CHUNKY GREEN APPLESAUCE

6–8 (about 2 pounds) summer   ½ cup sugar (about)
   apples*

Peel, core, and cut the apples into quarters. Place in a heavy saucepan and add just enough water to keep from scorching.

Cover and cook over medium heat, stirring occasionally until the apples are tender (about 15 to 20 minutes).

Break up the quarters to the desired size and stir in sugar to taste. Heat until the sugar dissolves. Serve warm or cold. Serves 6.

*Summer apples are tart cooking apples that are green or yellowish in color and somewhat small.

APPLE SNOW

2–3 apples   ⅛ teaspoon salt
  1 tablespoon lemon juice   ¼ cup sugar
  1 egg white

Peel the apples and grate enough to fill 1 cup. Put into a bowl and immediately stir in the lemon juice to prevent them from turning brown.

Beat the egg white with the salt until soft peaks form. Gradually beat in the sugar. Beat until almost stiff, then slowly beat in the grated apples and continue beating until stiff and glossy.

Pile into sherbet glasses and serve immediately. Serves 3 or 4.

COCOA PEARS WITH BRANDY SAUCE

The flavors of the pears and the chocolate combine to form a delightful taste.

1 cup sugar
1 cup water
½ teaspoon vanilla
4 ripe, but firm, fresh pears
4 rounded teaspoons cocoa

Brandy Sauce (recipe
follows)
Grated chocolate
(optional)

Combine the sugar, water, and vanilla in a skillet large enough to arrange the pear halves in one layer. Stir over low heat until the sugar dissolves and comes to a boil. Boil for 3 minutes.

Peel the pears, cut in half, and remove the cores with a measuring teaspoon. Simmer in the syrup, covered, for 10 to 15 minutes, or until tender, turning and basting occasionally. Remove from the heat and cool the pears in the syrup.

Drain the pears, leaving a little syrup in the cavities of 4 of the pear halves. Fill each cavity with a rounded teaspoon of cocoa. Top with the remaining pear halves, fastening together with picks to form 4 whole pears. Chill for at least 1 hour to allow the cocoa to form a syrup.

To serve, spoon the Brandy Sauce equally into 4 dessert dishes. Remove the picks from the pears and set into the sauce. If desired, garnish the tops with a few slivers of grated chocolate. Serves 4.

Brandy Sauce

1 egg yolk
1 tablespoon melted butter
1 cup sifted confectioners'
  sugar

1 tablespoon brandy
½ cup heavy cream

Beat the egg yolk slightly. Stir in the melted butter, then the confectioners' sugar and brandy. Chill.

Whip the cream until stiff. Fold it into the chilled brandy mixture.

Note: The sauce may be made several hours in advance and chilled.

FRESH PEARS WITH BUTTERED WINE SAUCE

4 ripe fresh pears*
  Lemon juice

    BUTTERED WINE SAUCE
½ cup butter

1 tablespoon cornstarch
2 tablespoons sugar
1 cup Port or Madeira wine
½ teaspoon lemon extract

Peel the pears, then core them from the bottom, leaving the stem intact. (If preferred, they need not be cored.) Rub with lemon juice to prevent discoloration.

Set the pears upright in dessert bowls or sherbet glasses.

To make the sauce, melt the butter in the top of a double boiler. Combine the cornstarch and sugar. Gradually stir in the wine, then the melted butter. Return to the double boiler.

Cook over direct heat, stirring constantly until the mixture comes to a boil and is clear. Cover and set over hot water until ready to serve then stir in the lemon extract.

Pour the wine sauce over the pears. Serves 4.

Note: The sauce may be served as soon as it is prepared. The double boiler is a convenience for advance preparation.

    *Bartlett or Bosc pears have tapered necks and the best shape.

CRANBERRY FLUMMERY

Flummeries are simply cornstarch puddings that date to Colonial days, and to England before that. They are made with fruit juices and occasionally with whole berries, as is the one selected here. The word "flummery" has also been used in the past to describe other soft fruit puddings similarly thickened.

2 cups cranberries
2¼ cups water
3 tablespoons cornstarch

1 cup sugar
⅛ teaspoon salt
Dairy sour cream

Rinse the cranberries and pick over, discarding any stems or soft berries.

Place the cranberries in a saucepan and add 2 cups of water. Bring to a boil, then cook for 5 minutes, or until the skins have popped.

Dissolve the cornstarch in the remaining ¼ cup of water. Gradually stir into the hot cranberries. Add the sugar and salt. Bring to a boil, cooking until thickened and clear.

Turn into a bowl. Cover and chill.

To serve, spoon out into sherbet glasses and top each with a spoonful of sour cream. Serves 6.

GRAPES WITH BROWN SUGAR AND SOUR CREAM

A dessert without a name. It is simple, attractive, and delicious.

3 cups (about ¾ pound) seedless green grapes	1 cup sour cream Dark brown sugar

Pull the grapes from the stems. Rinse and dry the grapes on paper toweling.

Combine the grapes with the sour cream, tossing lightly with a spoon until they are evenly coated. Spoon them into sherbet glasses and chill.

To serve, sprinkle the grapes with brown sugar, using about 2 teaspoons for each serving. Serves 4.

FRUIT IN SOUR CREAM

2 cups orange sections 2 bananas, peeled and sliced ½ inch thick 1 unpeeled red apple, diced	1 cup dairy sour cream Brown sugar Grated orange rind

Combine the oranges, bananas, and apple. Chill. Serve topped with sour cream, a sprinkle of brown sugar, and grated orange rind. Serves 6.

WINTER FRUIT CUP

3 oranges
1 grapefruit
¼ cup sugar

2 bananas
Sour Cream Sauce (recipe
follows)

Peel the oranges, removing all the white spongy exterior. Cut between the membranes to section. Repeat the process with the grapefruit. Combine the fruit sections with the sugar and chill thoroughly.

When ready to serve, drain the citrus, then slice the bananas and carefully mix in. Spoon into sherbet glasses and top with the hot Sour Cream Sauce. Serves 6.

Sour Cream Sauce

4 tablespoons butter
½ cup light brown sugar
(packed)

1 cup dairy sour cream
1 teaspoon vanilla

Melt the butter in a saucepan. Add the brown sugar. Cook over low heat, stirring until the sugar is dissolved. Stir in the sour cream and vanilla. Continue cooking just long enough to heat the cream. (Do not allow it to boil, or the cream will curdle.) Use immediately, or keep warm over hot water.

GLAZED ORANGES

4 large seedless oranges
1 cup sugar
½ cup water
¼ teaspoon orange or lemon
extract

Whipped cream or ice
cream (optional)

With a vegetable peeler, trim the zest from 1 orange (the orange part, not the spongy white). Cut enough of the zest into fine, long strips to make 2 tablespoons. Set aside.

Peel the oranges over a bowl (to retain all the juices), removing all the spongy white part. Cut between the membranes to section, dropping the sections into the bowl.

Drain the juice into a saucepan. Add the peel (zest), sugar, and water. Bring to a boil over medium heat, stirring until the sugar is dissolved. Continue boiling for 6 to 8 minutes, without stirring, until the syrup is thick. Stir in the orange or lemon extract.

Pour the hot syrup (with peel) over the orange sections. Refrigerate until thoroughly chilled.

Serve on dessert plates, plain or with whipped cream or over ice cream. Serves 4.

AMBROSIA

A Southern favorite, often served during the Christmas holidays.

8 seedless oranges
½ cup sugar
2 cups freshly grated coconut*

½ cup dry sherry

Peel the oranges, removing all the spongy white part. Cut in half from the blossom end, then slice ¼ inch thick.

Arrange a layer of orange slices in a glass or crystal serving bowl. Sprinkle with a little of the sugar, then add a layer of coconut. Repeat the layers, ending with coconut. Pour the sherry over all. Cover and chill for at least 1 hour (overnight if preferred).

Serve in sherbet glasses with a little of the sherry syrup spooned over each serving. Serves 8 to 10.

*See page 95 for the method of preparing fresh coconut.

A DISH OF SNOW
Grate the white part of cocoa-nut, put in a glass dish, and serve with oranges sliced and sugared, or with currant or cranberry jellies.

—Miss Beecher's Housekeeper and Healthkeeper
by Catharine E. Beecher (1873)

MELON BALL COMPOTE

2 cups cantaloupe balls	Wine Sauce (recipe follows)
2 cups honeydew melon balls	Mint for garnish (optional)
1 pint blueberries	

Prepare the melon balls, using a melon ball cutter or a measuring teaspoon. Chill thoroughly. Rinse the blueberries. Pick over and discard any stems or soft berries. Let stand at room temperature until ready to serve, then combine with the melon balls.

Serve in sherbet glasses. Pour the Wine Sauce over the tops. Garnish with sprigs of mint if desired. Serves 6.

Wine Sauce

⅓ cup honey	6–8 mint leaves
½ cup water	1 tablespoon lemon juice
¼ teaspoon salt	½ cup Port or Madeira wine

Combine the honey, water, salt, and mint leaves in a small saucepan. Bring to a boil, then simmer for 5 minutes. Cool and strain. Stir in the lemon juice and wine. Serve at room temperature.

FRIED BANANAS

A simple New Orleans specialty, not to be confused with the more elaborate Bananas Foster.

4 large, firm bananas	Flour
Lemon juice	2 tablespoons butter
Salt	Confectioners' sugar

Peel the bananas. Cut in half, then split lengthwise to make 4 sections each. Brush with lemon juice and sprinkle each very lightly with salt. Dip them into flour, shaking off the excess.

Melt the butter in a large skillet. Add the banana sections and sauté over medium-high heat for 1 or 2 minutes on each side, or until lightly browned and barely tender.

Remove the sections with a spatula and place directly onto individual serving plates. Sprinkle lightly with confectioners' sugar and serve immediately. Serves 4.

SUMMER FRUIT CUP

1½ quarts prepared fresh
    fruits*
1½ cups sugar

1 cup water
Juice and grated rind of 1
    lemon

Combine ½ to 1½ cups each of the selected prepared fruits to make 1½ quarts combined, using a minimum of four fruits. Choose for variety in color, texture, and flavor. The fruits should be fully ripe. Rinse and pick over for perfect quality before preparing.

Combine the sugar and water in a saucepan. Cook, stirring until the sugar is dissolved and the mixture comes to a boil. Boil without stirring for 5 minutes. Remove from the heat and stir in the lemon juice and rind. Cool until slightly warm, then strain through a fine sieve.

Pour the warm syrup over the prepared fruits. Chill thoroughly. Serve in a glass bowl or individual sherbets. Serves 6 to 8.

*Strawberries, halved or quartered if large
Raspberries (red or black) or blackberries
Blueberries
Grapes, halved and seeded if necessary
Peaches, peeled, pitted, and sliced
Apricots, peeled, pitted, and quartered
Pears, peeled, cored, and quartered or sliced
Plums (any variety), peeled, pitted, and quartered
Sweet cherries, pitted
Bananas, peeled and sliced
Avocados, peeled, pitted, and cubed
  Note: If bananas or avocados are selected, add to the fruit mixture just before serving.

STEWED RHUBARB

1 pound fresh rhubarb   Light cream (optional)
1½ cups sugar

Trim the leaves and stem ends from the rhubarb. Do not peel. Wash, then cut into 1-inch pieces across the stalks. There should be 3 cups. Put into a saucepan with the sugar. Mix and let stand for 15 minutes to draw the juices.

Cover and simmer until just tender (15 to 20 minutes). Do not add water and do not overcook.

Cool. Serve in sauce dishes or sherbet glasses, plain or with light cream. Serves 4.

STEWED BLUEBERRIES

2½ cups (1 pint) blueberries   1 teaspoon lemon juice
½ cup brown sugar (packed)   1 tablespoon butter
⅛ teaspoon salt   Vanilla ice cream

Rinse the berries and remove bits of stems and any soft berries. Drain.

Put the berries into a saucepan and add the brown sugar, salt, and lemon juice. Cook over low heat until the mixture comes to a boil, then boil for 1 minute. Remove from the heat, then stir in the butter.

Cool to room temperature. Serve over vanilla ice cream. Serves 6.

SUMMER PUDDING

Borrowed from the English, and traditionally made with red currants and raspberries that were picked at the same time in midsummer, this dessert was adopted by early New England settlers. Any juicy berry may be used for this unbaked bread pudding.

1 quart strawberries
1 cup sugar
½ teaspoon cinnamon
2 teaspoons lemon juice

10–12 slices white bread*
4 tablespoons melted butter
Heavy cream

Rinse the strawberries, remove the hulls, and slice into a bowl. Add the sugar, cinnamon, and lemon juice. Mix well, then let stand for 15 minutes to draw the juices, stirring occasionally.

Trim the crusts from the bread and discard. Brush one side of each slice with the melted butter.

Line the bottom and sides of a 1½-quart soufflé dish or casserole with the bread, buttered sides in, cutting the slices to fit. Pour half the strawberries and juice over the bread, add a layer of bread, and the remaining berries and juice. Top with the remaining bread, buttered sides down, also cut to fit.

Cover with a plate that will fit inside the bowl and place a weight on top. Refrigerate for at least 6 hours, or overnight, to allow the juices to soak through the bread.

To serve, unmold in a serving dish with a rimmed edge. Serve with unwhipped heavy cream. Serves 6.

*Firm, thin sandwich-type bread is preferred.

Fresh fruits, if thoroughly ripe, are more palatable and more healthful than if cooked. They should be looked over and sorted carefully. Reserve the finest for immediate table use, and put aside the bruised and imperfect to be cooked as soon as possible. Unless positive decay has set in, they may be stewed, and utilized in various ways.
—Mrs. Owens' Cook Book and Useful Household Hints
by Frances E. Owens, 1888 Revised Edition (1884)

BERRY FOOL

Credit for the Fool goes to the English. Traditionally it is made with gooseberries, but nearly any berry is suitable. The name comes from the Old French *fol*, meaning "crazy." This simple dessert consists of a puree of fresh berries folded into whipped cream; even a fool can do it.

1 quart ripe gooseberries, strawberries, blackberries, or raspberries	1 cup sugar (or more) ¼ cup water 2 cups heavy cream

Rinse the berries and remove the stems or hulls. Set aside a few for garnish (unless gooseberries are used, which must be cooked).

Slice the gooseberries or strawberries, but leave the other berries whole. Combine with the sugar and water in a saucepan. Cook slowly until tender (10 to 15 minutes), stirring frequently and pressing down with a fork to extract the juices. Taste and add additional sugar if preferred.

Press the cooked berries through a food mill or a coarse sieve. Chill the puree.

Just before serving, whip the cream until stiff and fold into the chilled puree. Spoon into a serving bowl or sherbet glasses. Garnish with the reserved berries. Serves 8.

HUCKLEBERRIES WITH CRACKERS AND CREAM

Pick over carefully one quart of blueberries, and keep them on ice until wanted. Put into each bowl, for each guest, two soda-crackers, broken in not too small pieces; add a few tablespoonfuls of berries, a teaspoonful of powdered sugar, and fill the bowl with the richest of cold, sweet cream. This is an old-fashioned New England breakfast dish. It also answers for a dessert.

—The White House Cook Book
by Mrs. F. L. Gillette and Hugo Ziemann, 1890 Edition (1887)

TUTTI-FRUTTI

Fermented fruits, popularly known as Tutti-Frutti, are an old-fashioned idea. Originally the dish consisted of a combination of fruits mixed with sugar, set away, and allowed to ferment naturally. The process was started in early summer and added to as new fruits came in season. It was ready to use about a month after the last fruit was added. By using fruits that are in season at the same time, and by adding brandy to accelerate the fermentation, you can shorten the process to about a week.

1 pint strawberries	3 cups sugar
1 pint red raspberries or blackberries	½ cup brandy
1 pint dark sweet cherries or sour red cherries	Ice cream, pudding, or unfrosted cake

Rinse the fruits and drain. Remove the hulls from the strawberries. Pick over and discard the stems and any bruised fruit. Leave the fruits whole.

Arrange the fruits alternately with the sugar in a stone crock or a widemouthed jar. Pour the brandy over the top. Cover loosely with a lid or foil and let stand in a cool place.

Stir carefully after 3 days to distribute the sugar, then daily until it is completely dissolved and forms a syrup. During this time, when the fruits begin to float, cover them with a plate and a nonmetal weight to keep them submerged.

When the juices cease to bubble (in about a week), the tutti-frutti is ready to use. Seal and refrigerate, where it will keep indefinitely.

Serve hot or cold over ice cream, puddings, or unfrosted cake.

STRAWBERRY FLOAT

A mound of meringue with sliced strawberries floating in pink cream.

1 quart strawberries	4 egg whites
1 cup sugar	¼ teaspoon salt
1 cup heavy cream	½ cup confectioners' sugar

Rinse the strawberries and remove the hulls. Slice into a bowl. Add the sugar and stir lightly. Let stand for at least 2 hours at room temperature to extract the juice. (The berries should be very soft.) Strain through a sieve, retaining both the berries and the juice.

Stir the juice into the heavy cream. Refrigerate if not using immediately.

Beat the egg whites with the salt until soft peaks form, then gradually beat in the confectioners' sugar. Beat until stiff peaks form, but the whites are not dry. Fold in the reserved sliced berries.

To serve, pour the pink cream into a glass or crystal bowl. Heap the meringue high upon it in the center, leaving a moat of the cream showing around the meringue.

When serving, spoon the meringue into individual sherbets, then spoon the pink cream over the tops of each. Serves 6.

STRAWBERRIES WITH POURING CUSTARD

In place of cream, chilled custard sauce is poured over perfect strawberries to make this simple, but delicious, dessert.

3 pints fresh strawberries	⅔ cup sugar
4 cups milk	1½ teaspoons vanilla
6 egg yolks	

Dip the strawberries in and out of cold water to rinse. Drain in a colander, then remove the hulls.

Heat the milk in a heavy saucepan until bubbles appear around the edge.

Beat the egg yolks with the sugar just enough to blend. Gradually pour in the hot milk, stirring constantly.

Set the saucepan over medium heat. Stir slowly until the mixture begins to thicken, then turn the heat to low and stir more rapidly until the sauce is thick enough to coat a clean metal spoon with a thin, creamy layer of sauce.

Note: At first the mixture will foam, then, as it gradually gets hotter, the bubbles will subside. Just before it thickens, a stream of vapor will rise. The gentle heat is necessary at this point or the eggs will overcook and curdle, instead of gradually turning into a smooth, velvety sauce.

Remove from the heat and stir the custard rapidly to bring the temperature down slightly. Stir in the vanilla. Cover and cool the custard, then chill thoroughly.

To serve, place the strawberries in individual dessert bowls. Pass the custard to pour over them. Serves 8 to 10.

DIPPED STRAWBERRIES

When full-flavored homegrown strawberries are in season, this is a perfect way to serve them.

2–3 pints strawberries*   **Unsifted confectioners' sugar**

Pick over and select only those berries that are perfect and of uniform size. Rinse quickly in cold water, then drain. Do not remove the hulls.

For each serving, press confectioners' sugar into a cordial or shot glass. Unmold in the center of each dessert plate.

Arrange the strawberries (10 to 12 for each serving) around the mound of sugar, stem ends toward the edge of the plates.

Dip the strawberries into the sugar with the fingers before eating. Serves 4 to 6.

*Since berry boxes are packed with strawberries of varying size, more strawberries than will be used for this dessert are suggested.

STRAWBERRY WHIP

1 cup sliced fresh
   strawberries
½ cup sugar

1 egg white
Sponge cake or other
   unfrosted cake

Rinse the strawberries and remove the hulls. Slice the berries and put into the bowl of an electric mixer. Add the sugar. Mix well, then let stand until the juices are drawn (about 30 minutes). Stir to dissolve the sugar.

Add the unbeaten egg white. Whip the mixture until stiff and glossy. (It will whip into a full quart.)

Serve over slices of the cake. Serves 8 or 10.

FRESH PEACHES WITH RUM CUSTARD

1½ cups milk
¼ cup light brown sugar
   (packed)
⅛ teaspoon salt

3 egg yolks
2 tablespoons dark rum
4 large fresh peaches

Combine the milk, brown sugar, and salt in the top of a double boiler. Heat slowly, stirring until bubbles appear around the edge and the sugar is dissolved.

Beat the egg yolks slightly. Gradually stir part of the milk and sugar mixture into the yolks, then return to the remainder. Cook over simmering water for about 20 minutes, stirring constantly until the mixture will coat a clean metal spoon. (Do not allow it to boil.)

Cool slightly, then stir in the rum. Cover and cool to room temperature, then chill thoroughly.

When ready to serve, scald the peaches in boiling water to loosen the skins, then peel. Cut each peach in half and place 2 halves in each of 4 sherbet glasses. Pour the custard over the tops. Serves 4.

PEACHES WITH RASPBERRY SYRUP

When peaches are served over ice cream with a puree of fresh raspberries, the dessert is known as Peach Melba. The original version was created by the famous French chef Escoffier in the late 1800s in honor of the great Austrian singer, Dame Nellie Melba. The classic version was garnished with almonds.

1 cup sugar	4 large ripe peaches
1 cup water	1 pint fresh red raspberries
½ teaspoon vanilla	Vanilla ice cream (optional)

Combine the sugar, water, and vanilla in a skillet large enough to arrange the peach halves in one layer. Stir over low heat until the sugar dissolves and comes to a boil. Boil for 3 minutes.

Dip the peaches into boiling water to cover for about 30 seconds to loosen the skins. Cool in cold water. Remove the skins, cut the peaches in half, and remove the pits. As they are prepared, put them into salt water (1 teaspoon to 1 quart) to prevent darkening, then transfer to the hot syrup.

Simmer the peaches in the syrup, covered, for 5 to 7 minutes, or until tender. Remove them with a slotted spoon to a colander to drain, then chill. Reserve the syrup.

Add the raspberries to the syrup, reserving a few for garnish. Bring to a boil, then turn the heat to low and allow the mixture to bubble slowly, uncovered, until thick and syrupy (about 5 to 10 minutes).

Line a sieve with a double thickness of rinsed cheesecloth and set it over a bowl. Pour the berries and syrup into the sieve and allow to drain briefly. Then twist the cloth and press lightly with a spoon to extract the remaining juice. Discard the berries and chill the syrup.

To serve, spoon the raspberry syrup over the peach halves and scatter the reserved berries over the top; or place a scoop of vanilla ice cream on each peach half and top with the syrup and berries. Serves 4 plain with two peach halves per serving, or 8 with ice cream and one peach half.

FRIED PEACHES

A Southern specialty.

4 large, firm peaches	Heavy cream or ice cream
4 tablespoons butter	(optional)
6 tablespoons sugar	

Peel and halve the peaches. Remove and discard the pits.

Melt the butter in a heavy skillet just enough to arrange the peach halves in one layer. Lay the peach halves, cavities down, in the butter. Sauté over low heat until the edges are lightly browned.

Turn the peaches and sprinkle with half the sugar, then turn again and sprinkle with the remaining sugar. Continue cooking until the peaches are tender and the sugar has melted and caramelized slightly. Baste occasionally as the sugar melts.

Serve warm with the caramelized sauce, or, if desired, also with heavy cream, whipped or unwhipped, or ice cream. Serves 4.

POACHED FRUIT COMPOTE

The advantage of preparing a fruit compote with fresh fruits is that they have a firmer texture and a more natural flavor than most fruits that come from cans. The plums release their color when cooked, providing an attractive red syrup that is served over the poached fruit.

1½ cups sugar	3 fresh pears or 6 Seckel
2 cups water	pears
2 teaspoons vanilla	6 fresh apricots
3 fresh peaches	6 fresh prune plums

Combine the sugar, water, and vanilla in a large skillet. Bring to a boil over medium heat, stirring until the sugar is dissolved. Boil for 3 minutes, then remove from the heat.

Dip the peaches into boiling water to cover for about 30 seconds to loosen the skins. Cool in cold water, then remove the skins. Cut the peaches in half and remove the pits. As they are prepared, put them into salt water (1 teaspoon to 1 quart) to prevent darkening.

*Ice cream made with fresh fruit,
or a sundae—take your pick:
a scoop of mouth-watering Fresh Strawberry Ice Cream
or satisfyingly rich American Vanilla Ice Cream
with Caramel Syrup (page 222).*

Peel the pears; dip them into salt water to prevent discoloration. Cut them in half and remove the cores and stems. (If using Seckel pears, leave them whole with the stem intact.)

Rinse the apricots. Do not peel them; leave them whole.

Add the peaches, pears, and apricots to the syrup. Cover and bring to a boil, then simmer, basting occasionally, until barely tender (5 to 7 minutes). They should remain slightly firm. Check the fruits at minimum time by piercing with a fork. The length of cooking time will depend on the degree of ripeness.

Remove the fruits with a slotted spoon and place in a bowl. Pour less than half the syrup over the fruit. Set aside to cool, basting occasionally.

Add the whole, unpeeled plums to the remaining syrup. Cook, turning until they split open. Transfer to a second bowl and pour the syrup over them.

Allow the fruit to cool, then chill in the syrup. (The plums must be stored separately to prevent staining the other fruits.)

Remove the fruit from the refrigerator before serving so that it is not icy cold.

To serve, drain the fruit, reserving the syrup from the plums. Arrange the fruit attractively in a large glass or crystal bowl or individual bowls. Pour the plum syrup over the top. Each portion should contain a peach half, a pear half (or a whole Seckel pear), an apricot, and a plum. Serves 6.

There was a time, and not so very long ago either, when we looked upon fruits as luxuries and food accessories rather than considering them as a vital and necessary part of our daily diet. That was probably due to two or three reasons; first, fruits were less plentiful; second, they were very much more expensive; third, we knew comparatively little about them.

—The Menu Book of the American Housewife
(1929)

PEACH CRISP

Apple Crisp is the most familiar member of this old-fashioned family of desserts, but peaches and rhubarb were prepared in the same way, often with an undercrust of pastry.

½ cup sugar	½ teaspoon salt
4 cups (2 pounds) sliced fresh peaches	½ teaspoon cinnamon
1 cup sifted all-purpose flour	½ cup soft butter
½ cup brown sugar (packed)	Light or heavy cream (optional)

Add the sugar to the sliced peaches and mix lightly. Place in a buttered 1½-quart shallow baking dish.

Combine the flour, brown sugar, salt, and cinnamon in a mixing bowl. Cut in the soft butter with a fork or with your fingers until crumbly.

Sprinkle the crumbs over the peaches. Bake in a 350° oven until the peaches are tender and the top is crispy and golden brown (about 40 minutes).

Serve warm, plain or with light or heavy cream poured over the top. Serves 6.

VI

Ice Cream, Ices, and Other Frozen Desserts

FROM ENGLAND the Colonists brought the formula for making ice cream, or milk ice as it was first known. It has been a strong favorite since that time and today stands as something of an American symbol.

In history ice cream dates to the thirteenth century, when Marco Polo returned to Italy from the Orient with tales of men eating ices flavored with exotic fruits. Ices were popular in Italy from the fourteenth century on. It was an Italian confectioner who introduced the idea to the French in 1660. The French reportedly added milk, a variation that was then copied by the English.

In the late 1700s George Washington and Thomas Jefferson helped popularize ice cream in America. But until Dolley Madison put it on the White House menu as dessert, it was considered a confection.

The first ice-cream freezer suitable for family use was invented in 1846. Before that ice cream was made in an "ice pot." A bowl containing the cream mixture was set into a pot filled with ice. The mixture was stirred until it thickened, then spun in the ice until it froze.

Homemade ice cream had its heyday in the Victorian era around the turn of the twentieth century, when ice cream socials were a part of the American way of life. After that, interest dwindled. When the electric refrigerator with its freezing compartment was in common use in the 1930s and 1940s, and recipes were adapted for its use, interest in ice-cream making revived.

Current enthusiasm for churned homemade ice cream has returned as a result of the electrification of the old-time ice-cream freezer. The process is now quite simple.

Freezing Directions for Hand-Crank or Electric Freezer

Ice-cream mixtures (ices and sherbets) should be frozen according to the directions provided with either type of machine. For the finest quality, the following additional suggestions and procedure may be helpful.

1. The ice-cream mixture must be thoroughly chilled before freezing, or it may turn buttery or coarse. If heavy cream is to be whipped, it should be beaten only until it mounds lightly, not until stiff (this gives the ice cream a light, delicate texture). Fruits and coarsely chopped nuts and liquors should be added halfway through the freezing process, since they slow the freezing of the cream mixture.

2. The freezer can, dasher, and lid should be washed with soapy hot water, rinsed and dried, then chilled.

3. The following process should be used for freezing and ripening the frozen mixture.

a. Use finely crushed ice and either rock salt or kosher salt in a 6-to-1 proportion by weight (1½ quarts of ice to ½ cup of salt). Table salt melts too rapidly to produce the best results. If too much salt is used, the ice cream will be granular.

b. Pour the chilled ice-cream mixture into the chilled can and set in the freezer; cover and let stand for 5 minutes after packing with salt and ice. The freezer can should be filled no more than two-thirds full to allow for expansion, or the ice cream will be granular.

c. To pack the freezer, add a 2-inch layer of ice, sprinkle about 3 tablespoons of salt over the ice, then pack down. Continue to build layers this way until the level is above the level of the ice-cream mixture. As the ice melts and a brine forms, add more salt and ice.

d. For a hand-cranked freezer, turn the crank slowly until the mixture starts to freeze. (This will ensure a smooth, fine-grained product.) Then turn it rapidly until the crank is very difficult to turn.

e. Whenever removing the lid (for checking, to add additional ingredients, or when the ice cream is frozen), wipe it off so that no brine gets into the ice cream.

f. When the ice cream is frozen, pour off the brine and repack in a 4-to-1 proportion by weight (1 quart of ice to ½ cup of salt). Cover with the lid, then cover the can with a heavy towel and let it stand for 1 to 2 hours to ripen. This will harden the ice cream and improve the flavor.

g. The ice cream may also be ripened in a food freezer. Remove the can from the freezer bucket and cover as above; or spoon into plastic containers, allowing ½ inch for expansion. Pack the ice down and cover with tight-fitting lids.

Note: Sherbets and ices are frozen in the same manner, but more salt in proportion to the ice should be used. (Use a 4-to-1 ice to salt ratio by weight, or 1 quart of ice to ½ cup of salt.)

Refrigerator Ice Cream, Sherbet, or Ice

Although any mixture to be frozen may be frozen in the freezer compartment of a refrigerator or a deep freezer, for best quality and smooth texture the mixture should contain gelatin, whipped egg whites, whipped cream, syrup, or other ingredients that provide body and help prevent crystallization.

For this reason, they must also be stirred, then beaten, partway through the freezing process.

Here are some suggestions.

1. The freezer control should be set for fast freezing.

2. The refrigerator tray should first be rinsed on the outside with cold water, filled, and placed in the bottom of the freezing compartment to facilitate rapid freezing.

3. The mixture should be stirred several times. When it is partially frozen and has a mushy consistency, it should be beaten in a chilled bowl with a rotary or electric beater. (If it is beaten too soon, it will return to its original liquid state.) After that it should be stirred occasionally until solidly frozen.

4. The freezer container should be filled no more than three-fourths full, since the stirring or beating whips in air and causes the mixture to increase in bulk.

Frozen Desserts

Any frozen dessert with a mixture containing a large percentage of whipped cream that is added when preparing the mixture, not later, may be frozen in a refrigerator freezer compartment or a deep freezer without additional stirring or beating.

PHILADELPHIA ICE CREAM

Philadelphia was famous for its commercially made ice cream from the late 1700s through the nineteenth century and the beginning of the twentieth century. The ice cream known as Philadelphia Ice Cream is made from sweetened and flavored pure cream without the addition of eggs or other thickeners.

4 cups light cream, chilled	**¼ teaspoon salt**
¾ cup sugar	**1 tablespoon vanilla**

Method I: Combine the cream with the sugar and salt, stirring until the sugar is dissolved (about 5 minutes). Stir in the vanilla. (The cream increases considerably in volume, and the ice cream has a light, snowy texture.)

Method II: Heat the cream until bubbles appear around the edge. Add the sugar and salt, stirring to dissolve. Cool, then add the vanilla. Refrigerate until thoroughly chilled. (This method produces ice cream that is smooth and velvety with a rich body and flavor.)

Freeze in an ice-cream freezer according to Freezing Directions for Hand-Crank or Electric Freezer, page 213. Makes about 1½ quarts.

Note: These ice creams are light in texture and should be consumed shortly after preparing. Stored in the freezer, they become unpleasantly hard.

PURE ICE CREAM

Genuine ice-cream is made of the pure sweet cream in this proportion: Two quarts of cream, one pound of sugar; beat up, flavor, and freeze.

For family use, select one of the new patent freezers, as being more rapid and less laborious for small quantities than the old style turned entirely by hand. All conditions being perfect, those with crank and revolving dashers effect freezing in eight to fifteen minutes.

—The White House Cook Book
by Mrs. F. L. Gillette and Hugo Ziemann, 1890 Edition (1887)

PISTACHIO ICE CREAM

A variation of Philadelphia Ice Cream.

½ cup shelled pistachios	¼ teaspoon salt
½ cup shelled almonds	2 teaspoons almond extract
4 cups light cream	Green food coloring
1 cup sugar	

Place the pistachios and almonds in a saucepan. Cover with water and bring to a boil. Drain in a colander. While warm, pinch off the skins. Chop fine and set aside.

Heat the cream until bubbles appear around the edge. Remove from the heat and add the sugar and salt, stirring until dissolved. Cool, then stir in the almond extract. Add a few drops of green food coloring to tint the mixture a delicate green color. Refrigerate until thoroughly chilled.

Pour the chilled cream mixture into the freezer can of an ice-cream freezer and freeze according to Freezing Directions for Hand-Crank or Electric Freezer, page 213, until partially frozen. Stir in the pistachios and almonds and continue freezing. Makes about 1¾ quarts.

PEPPERMINT STICK ICE CREAM

The candy sweetens, colors, and flavors the ice-cream mixture so that only milk and cream are required. Although whipping the cream is not necessary, it makes the ice cream lighter in texture.

½ pound peppermint stick candy canes	2 cups milk
	2 cups heavy cream

Crush the candy canes. (It is easy to do if the broken sticks are pulverized in a blender.)

Heat the milk until bubbles appear around the edge. Remove from the heat and add the crushed candy, stirring until the candy is dissolved. Chill thoroughly.

Whip the cream until it mounds lightly, not until stiff. Fold into the chilled candy mixture.

Pour the mixture into the freezer can of an ice-cream freezer and freeze according to Freezing Directions for Hand-Crank or Electric Freezer, page 213. Makes about 1½ quarts.

FRENCH VANILLA ICE CREAM

European in origin, this ice cream is made with a cooked custard base. It is rich and creamy.

1½ cups milk	3 egg yolks
¾ cup sugar	1 tablespoon vanilla
⅛ teaspoon salt	2 cups heavy cream

Heat the milk in a heavy saucepan until bubbles appear around the edge. Remove from the heat and add the sugar and salt, stirring until dissolved.

Beat the egg yolks slightly. Stir part of the milk mixture into the egg yolks. Add to the remainder and cook over low heat, stirring constantly until the mixture is slightly thickened and coats a clean metal spoon. (Do not let it boil, or it will curdle.) Remove from the heat and cool slightly before stirring in the vanilla. Strain, then cover and cool to room temperature. Chill thoroughly.

Whip the cream until it mounds lightly but is not stiff. Fold it into the chilled custard mixture.

Pour the mixture into the freezer can of an ice-cream freezer. Freeze according to Freezing Directions for Hand-Crank or Electric Freezer, page 213. Makes about 1½ quarts.

FROZEN EGGNOG

This dessert does not freeze as solidly as ice cream because of its alcoholic content.

2 cups milk	¼ cup bourbon whiskey
1 cup sugar	2 tablespoons rum
4 egg yolks	Sweetened whipped cream
1 teaspoon vanilla	and maraschino cherries
2 cups heavy cream	(optional)

Heat the milk with the sugar in a saucepan, stirring until the sugar is dissolved. Remove from the heat.

Beat the egg yolks until the mixture is thick and lemon-colored and falls back on itself in a ribbon when the beaters are raised. Slowly stir in about one-third of the hot milk mixture, then return to the heat. Cook, stirring over low heat until the mixture is lightly thickened and will coat a clean metal spoon. (Do not boil, or the mixture will curdle.) Remove from the heat and cool, then stir in the vanilla. Chill thoroughly.

Pour the chilled mixture into the freezer can and freeze according to Freezing Directions for Hand-Crank or Electric Freezer, page 213, until partly frozen.

Whip the cream until it mounds softly. Stir into the partly frozen mixture along with the whiskey and rum. Continue the freezing process until frozen.

To serve, spoon into parfait glasses, garnishing the tops with sweetened whipped cream and a maraschino cherry, if desired.

VARIOUS COLOURINGS FOR ICES, JELLIES, CREAMS, ETC.

A tincture made by pouring hot water over some sliced beet-root will give a beautiful red; or, boil a small quantity of cochineal finely powdered, with a drachm of cream of tartar to half a pint of water; to which add, when boiling, a very little bit of alum.

For white, use almond-paste or cream.

For yellow, tincture of saffron.

For green, the expressed juice of spinach-leaves.

—Modern American Cookery
by Miss Prudence Smith (1835)

BUTTER PECAN ICE CREAM

Another variation of ice cream based on custard sauce.

3 cups light cream	4 teaspoons vanilla
3 cups milk	4 teaspoons butter
1½ cups sugar	1 cup pecans
5 eggs	¼ teaspoon salt

Heat the cream and milk in a saucepan until bubbles appear around the edge. Remove from the heat.

Melt ½ cup of sugar in a small, heavy skillet, stirring occasionally until golden brown.

Gradually stir the caramelized sugar into the hot cream mixture. Stir over low heat until melted again.

Beat the eggs slightly. Gradually add the remaining cup of sugar. Stir part of the cream mixture into the eggs, then return to the remainder. Cook, stirring over low heat until the mixture will coat a clean metal spoon. (Do not boil.) Strain into a bowl, cool slightly, and stir in the vanilla. Cover and cool to room temperature, then chill thoroughly (at least 4 hours, or overnight).

Melt the butter in a small, heavy skillet over low heat. Add the pecans and stir until lightly toasted. Remove from the heat, chop coarsely, add the salt, and mix well. Set aside to cool.

Pour the cream mixture into the freezer can and freeze according to Freezing Directions for Hand-Crank or Electric Freezer, page 213, until partly frozen. Stir in the toasted pecans and continue the freezing process. Makes about 2½ quarts.

CHOCOLATE ALMOND ICE CREAM

Rich, chocolatey, and delicious.

3 1-ounce squares	⅛ teaspoon salt
unsweetened chocolate	1 cup milk
4 cups light cream	2 tablespoons vanilla
1½ cups sugar	1 cup blanched almonds
4 eggs	

Cut the chocolate into pieces and add 1 cup of the cream and the sugar. Heat, stirring occasionally until the chocolate is melted. Stir well until blended.

Beat the eggs and salt slightly. Gradually stir the chocolate mixture into the egg mixture, then return to the heat and cook, stirring constantly over low heat until the mixture will coat a spoon with a creamy film. Stir in the remaining 3 cups of cream, the milk, and the vanilla. Strain into a bowl, cover, and chill thoroughly.

Place the almonds in one layer in a dry, heavy skillet. Stir over low heat until light brown. Remove from the heat and cool. (Do not overbrown, since they continue to darken as they cool.) Chop coarsely and set aside.

Pour the chilled cream mixture into the freezer can and freeze according to Directions for Hand-Crank or Electric Freezer, page 213, until partially frozen. Stir in the toasted almonds and continue the freezing process. Makes about 2½ quarts.

In freezing creams of all sorts, and water, or fruit ices, the process is greatly simplified by having the ice crushed fine. Many cooks who are new to the business, do not recognize this fact. In consequence, they learn that to freeze cream takes very much longer than they were led to imagine from the circular advertising "the most rapid freezer, ever put upon the market." While this circular may to a certain extent exaggerate the facts, do not condemn the new machine until you have pounded or shaved your ice very fine. A machine for shaving ice facilitates this process. Lacking this, put the ice into a strong bag and pound it fine with a wooden mallet.

—Marion Harland's Complete Cook Book
1906 Revised Edition (1903)

AMERICAN VANILLA ICE CREAM

Ice cream called American contains eggs. It is similar to French ice cream, but is prepared without cooking. In addition, this type of ice cream is less rich.

2 cups milk	½ teaspoon salt
4 cups light cream	2 tablespoons vanilla
1 cup sugar	Caramel Syrup (recipe
2 eggs	follows)

Heat the milk, cream, and sugar in a heavy saucepan, stirring until the sugar is dissolved and bubbles appear around the edge. Remove from the heat.

Beat the eggs well. Gradually stir in the hot cream mixture. Cool slightly and stir in the salt and vanilla. Strain and chill.

Pour the mixture into the freezer can of an ice-cream freezer. Freeze according to Freezing Directions for Hand-Crank or Electric Freezer, page 213. Makes about 2 quarts. Serve with Caramel Syrup.

Caramel Syrup

½ cup sugar	½ cup boiling water

Put the sugar in a heavy skillet over low heat. Stir constantly until it has melted to a brown liquid. When it bubbles over the entire surface, remove from the heat. Add the boiling water very slowly, stirring constantly.

FRESH STRAWBERRY ICE CREAM

An American-type ice cream, this version is made with strawberry puree, strained so that the seeds are omitted.

1 quart ripe strawberries	1 cup heavy cream
2 tablespoons lemon juice	½ teaspoon salt
1½ cups sugar	2 eggs
3 cups light cream	2 teaspoons vanilla

Rinse, drain, and remove the hulls from the strawberries, cutting away any bruised or unripe parts. Slice, then crush thoroughly. Add the lemon juice and 1 cup of sugar. Let stand 1 to 2 hours to soften the berries and draw the juices.

Put the berries into a strainer lined with a square of rinsed cheesecloth and set over a bowl. Gather the edges of the cheesecloth, twist, and squeeze as long as any juice or pulp can be extracted. Chill the resulting puree.

Combine the light and heavy creams in a saucepan. Heat until bubbles appear around the edge. Remove from the heat, add the remaining ½ cup of sugar and the salt, and stir until dissolved. Cool.

Beat the eggs until light, then stir into the cream mixture. Stir in the strawberry puree and the vanilla, then chill thoroughly.

Pour the chilled mixture into the freezing can and freeze according to Freezing Directions for Hand-Crank or Electric Freezer, page 213. Makes 2 quarts.

When it is desired to have the cream in blocks or cakes a special mould will be needed. Any tinsmith will make a mould of block tin, with a water-tight cover, of any shape or size desired, if it is not obtainable at a hardware store. The mould should be set in ice and salt while the cream is being frozen, and when the beater or mixer is removed the cream should be packed down into the mould as quickly as possible. It should be pressed down firmly and smoothly and a piece of stout muslin or buttered paper laid over it before the mould cover is put on. The mould is then packed in ice and salt and kept for a few hours until the cream is ready for use.

—Butterick's "Correct Cookery"
(1900)

REFRIGERATOR VANILLA ICE CREAM

The addition of gelatin and whipped cream makes this Philadelphia-type ice cream suitable for freezing in the freezer compartment of a refrigerator.

2 teaspoons unflavored gelatin	1 cup sugar
¼ cup cold water	⅛ teaspoon salt
2 cups milk	1 tablespoon vanilla
	2 cups heavy cream

Sprinkle the gelatin over the cold water. Set aside to soften.

Heat the milk until bubbles appear around the edge. Remove from the heat. Add the softened gelatin, the sugar, and the salt and stir until dissolved. Cool, then blend in the vanilla.

Chill, stirring occasionally until the mixture mounds softly, then beat until light and fluffy.

Whip the cream until almost stiff. Fold into the gelatin mixture. Turn into a freezer tray (or trays), stirring occasionally, and freeze until firm. Cover airtight. Makes about 1½ quarts.

Note: If preferred, use a 9x9x2-inch baking pan or a 9x5x3-inch loaf pan for freezing.

FRESH PEACH ICE CREAM

Another ice cream suitable for freezing in a refrigerator freezer.

1 cup peeled, coarsely chopped fresh peaches	2 egg yolks
1 tablespoon lemon juice	½ cup sugar
¼ cup light corn syrup	⅛ teaspoon almond extract
1 cup light cream	2 egg whites

Combine the peaches, lemon juice, and corn syrup. Puree in a blender, then stir in the cream.

Beat the egg yolks slightly, then gradually beat in the sugar. Continue beating until thick and lemon-colored. Stir in the pureed peaches and the almond extract.

Freeze in a refrigerator freezer tray until a mushy consistency, stirring once or twice.

Turn the frozen mixture into a chilled bowl. Beat until smooth, then add the unbeaten egg whites and beat until smooth and fluffy.

Return to the refrigerator freezer tray. Freeze, stirring occasionally until firm, then cover airtight. Serves 6.

Note: This ice cream is pale in color. If desired, add a few drops of red and yellow food coloring before freezing.

GRAHAM CRACKER ICE CREAM

1 cup coarsely crushed graham crackers	2 cups light cream
½ cup sugar	1 teaspoon vanilla

Combine the graham cracker crumbs, sugar, cream, and vanilla. Stir until the sugar is dissolved.

Freeze in a refrigerator tray until the mixture has a mushy consistency, stirring once or twice.

Turn into a chilled bowl. Beat until smooth and fluffy. Return to the freezer tray and freeze until firm without stirring, then cover to prevent crystallization. Serves 4.

GRAPE SHERBET

Sherbets are frozen like ice cream, but are made with milk or diluted cream and fruit juices. They are lighter and less rich than ice cream. This one is a beautiful lilac color.

2 cups unsweetened grape juice	1 cup sugar
	4 cups milk

Heat the grape juice with the sugar, stirring until the sugar is dissolved. Cool.

Gradually stir the grape juice mixture into the milk. Chill thoroughly.

Freeze according to Freezing Directions for Hand-Crank or Electric Freezer, page 213. Makes about 2 quarts.

ORANGE SHERBET

This sherbet is made in the freezing compartment of a refrigerator.

1½ cups sugar	1½ cups orange juice
1½ cups water	4 tablespoons lemon juice
Grated rind of 1 orange	1½ cups heavy cream

Bring 1 cup of sugar and the water to a boil, stirring until the sugar is dissolved. Simmer for 5 minutes without stirring. Remove from the heat and pour over the grated orange rind. Let stand for 30 minutes.

Add the orange juice and lemon juice to the orange-flavored syrup, then strain.

Freeze in a refrigerator tray until it has a mushy consistency, stirring once or twice.

Whip the cream lightly, then beat in the remaining ½ cup of sugar. Continue beating until almost stiff.

Beat the fruit juice mixture until smooth and fluffy. Fold in the whipped cream and return to the freezer tray (or trays). Freeze, stirring occasionally until firm, then cover. Makes 1½ quarts.

Note: This sherbet is pale in color. If desired, add a few drops of red and yellow food coloring to the syrup mixture before freezing.

PINEAPPLE SHERBET

1½ teaspoons unflavored gelatin	1 9-ounce can crushed pineapple in heavy syrup
2 tablespoons cold water	1 teaspoon vanilla
2 cups buttermilk	1 egg white
1 cup plus 2 tablespoons sugar	

Soften the gelatin in the cold water, then dissolve over hot water.

Combine the buttermilk, 1 cup of sugar, the pineapple (with syrup) and the vanilla. Add the softened gelatin and stir until the sugar is dissolved.

Beat the egg white until soft peaks form. Gradually beat in the 2 tablespoons of sugar and continue beating until stiff. Fold into the gelatin mixture.

Turn into a refrigerator freezer tray and freeze until firm, stirring once or twice. When frozen, cover to prevent crystallization. Makes about 1 quart.

LEMON ICE

Ices are the simplest of frozen desserts. They are made with water, sugar, and fruit juices.

½ cup sugar cubes	1 cup boiling water
4 medium-size lemons	2 cups cold water
¾ cup sugar	

Rub the edges of the sugar cubes over the lemon skins to extract the oils. Squeeze the juice from the lemons and set aside.

Add the sugar cubes and ¾ cup of sugar to the boiling water and stir until dissolved. Add the cold water and the lemon juice. Strain into a bowl, then chill thoroughly.

Pour the chilled fruit juice mixture into the freezer can and freeze according to Freezing Directions for Hand-Crank or Electric Freezer, page 213. Makes about 1 quart.

Rub some sugar on lemon or orange-peel to give a flavour to the water, then squeeze the juice on its own peel, and add a sufficiency of sugar and water; strain the whole, and put it in the ice-pot; or, the water may be mixed with the strained juice of any kind of fruit agreeable to taste.

—Modern American Cookery
by Miss Prudence Smith (1835)

THREE OF A KIND

This fruit ice may be frozen in a refrigerator but will not be quite as good as that churned in an ice-cream freezer. It is an old-time favorite that has lasted through the years, possibly because the proportions are easy to remember.

3 oranges	3 cups sugar
3 lemons	3 cups water
3 bananas	3 egg whites

Squeeze the juice from the oranges and the lemons. Mash the bananas; combine with the juice and press through a wire strainer.

Combine the sugar and water in a saucepan. Heat, stirring until the sugar is dissolved, then remove from the heat and cool. Stir into the fruit mixture. Chill thoroughly.

Pour the chilled mixture into the freezer can and freeze according to Freezing Directions for Hand-Crank or Electric Freezer, page 213, until partly frozen.

Beat the egg whites until stiff but not dry. Stir into the partly frozen mixture. Continue the freezing process.

Note: If frozen in a refrigerator freezer, freeze until the mixture is a mushy consistency, stirring once or twice. Beat until fluffy, then fold in the beaten egg whites. Return to the freezer and freeze, stirring occasionally until firm.

Water ices are not so easy to make successfully, but with a little practice good results can be obtained. More salt and a longer freezing will be required than is needed for cream.

—Butterick's "Correct Cookery"
(1900)

FROZEN FRUITCAKE

This molded dessert, known also as Frozen Plum Pudding, contains a combination of macaroons, ladyfingers, nuts, and raisins. It was popular in the late 1800s in the South for weddings, receptions, and formal parties.

1 cup seedless raisins	12 ladyfingers
Sherry wine	1 cup finely chopped
4 cups milk	blanched almonds
1 cup sugar	2 cups heavy cream
4 eggs	Butter Wine Sauce (recipe
12 almond macaroons	follows)

Soak the raisins overnight in enough sherry wine to cover, then drain.

Heat the milk and sugar in a saucepan until bubbles appear around the edge, stirring until the sugar dissolves. Remove from the heat.

Beat the eggs slightly. Gradually stir in part of the milk. Return to the remainder and cook over low heat, stirring constantly until the mixture thickens slightly and will coat a spoon. (Do not boil, or the mixture will curdle.) Cover and cool to room temperature, then chill thoroughly.

Crumble the macaroons and break the ladyfingers into small pieces. Add to the chilled mixture along with the almonds and drained raisins.

Whip the cream until it mounds lightly but is not stiff. Fold into the chilled fruit mixture. Turn into a 2½-quart mold and cover securely to prevent crystallization.

Freeze until firm. Unmold and serve with Butter Wine Sauce if desired. Serves 12.

Butter Wine Sauce

1 cup butter	2 egg whites
2 cups sifted confectioners'	⅓ cup sherry
sugar	¼ cup boiling water

Beat the butter with the sugar until creamy. Add the unbeaten egg whites, the sherry, and the boiling water. Set in a pan of hot water and beat until smooth and frothy.

HEAVENLY HASH

18 almond macaroons	1½ cups sifted confectioners'
1 cup pecans	sugar
½ cup candied cherries	4 egg whites
4 cups heavy cream	⅛ teaspoon salt
1 teaspoon almond extract	

Break the macaroons into coarse crumbs. Chop the pecans and cherries coarsely.

Whip the cream until stiff, adding the almond extract toward the end of beating. Sift the confectioners' sugar over the top of the cream and fold in. Fold in the macaroon crumbs, pecans, and cherries.

Beat the egg whites with the salt until stiff but not dry. Fold into the cream mixture.

Turn into a 2-quart mold, cover securely to prevent crystallization, and freeze until firm.

CHOCOLATE BISCUIT

A frozen chocolate mousse garnished with macaroon crumbs.

2 1-ounce squares	6 egg yolks
unsweetened chocolate	1 teaspoon vanilla
¼ cup light cream	2 cups heavy cream
⅓ cup sugar	Macaroon crumbs
⅛ teaspoon salt	

Cut the chocolate into small pieces. Combine with the light cream, sugar, and salt in a heavy saucepan. Cook, stirring over low heat until the chocolate is melted and the sugar is dissolved. Cool.

Beat the egg yolks until thick and lemon-colored. Blend in the cooled chocolate mixture and the vanilla.

Whip the cream until almost stiff and fold into the chocolate mixture. Turn into a mold, cover tightly, and freeze without stirring until firm.

Unmold and garnish each serving with finely ground macaroon crumbs. Serves 8 to 10.

INDEX